T0196578

THE JOURNEY OF AN IMMIGRANT

FROM FARM TO FREEDOM

KHETAM DAHI

Order this book online at www.trafford.com
or email orders@trafford.com

Most Trafford titles are also available at major online book retailers.

Printed in the United States of America.

ISBN: 978-1-4669-4766-5 (sc)
ISBN: 978-1-4669-4767-2 (e)

Trafford rev. 07/13/2012

 www.trafford.com

North America & international
toll-free: 1 888 232 4444 (USA & Canada)
phone: 250 383 6864 ♦ fax: 812 355 4082

DEDICATION

To my husband, Ayham Dahi, my inspiration, supporter beyond limits, friend, soul mate, great role model and amazing father to our four children

NOTE TO THE READER

The stories you are about to read are mostly based on true situations that my family and I experienced when leaving our homeland, Syria and as immigrants in the USA. In some cases, I omitted or added information to protect some characters' privacy. I also changed most characters' names so as to not reveal personal information. The order of events may not be 100% accurate, but mostly true based on my memory. I tried to do my best to keep the stories as genuinely true as possible, but had to fill in the gaps creatively where needed.

I hope to entertain, inspire, motivate and intrigue you, share my positive and negative experiences with you as an immigrant, and hopefully bring awareness of many social issues, mistreatment and bad work conditions that immigrants have endured and still do.

Over the years, I have read hundreds of journal entries written by my ESL students, and they have often touched and inspired me, so they are a huge part of the reason why I am sharing my stories.

Please contact me for any helpful feedback on this first project as I am always learning and trying to improve my writing and teaching methods. Next, I will be working on a book based on my life on a farm in Syria, which will hopefully give more background knowledge about the culture, social issues, type of daily work and situations people had, and many anecdotes about my childhood as a farmer's daughter in the sixties and seventies. The name of my next book is *The Mulberry Tree: Stories of a Farm Girl*.

E-mail: dahik@elac.edu

Acknowledgements

I want to thank the following people for supporting me in doing this project: My husband Ayham Dahi, my biggest critic and supporter, Novia Elvina, our ESL Club Delegate, who did the majority of the cartoon illustrations inside the book, Sandro Wong and Cindy Liang, our East Los Angeles College ESL Club Presidents and Vice-President for being my right and left hands last semester as they ran most of the meetings and organized all the fundraisers for the club so that I could focus on teaching and writing, my daughter, Reem Atallah and her friend Mike Floresca for designing the book cover and organizing all the illustrations, my colleagues and friends, Dr. Linda Elias, Associate Professors Nancy Ramirez, Nathan Warner, and Arleta Roberts for their invaluable comments, suggestions, ideas and corrections. I am also grateful to my brother-in-law, Dr. Omar Dahi for doing much of the editing at such a short notice and for making many confusing parts a lot clearer, my brother Sam Atalla for proofreading and filling in some gaps when I did not remember details about some events, my four children, Kinda, Reem, Jamal and Joel for being patient and supportive in every way, and my nine wonderful brothers and sisters for their constant support. Most of all, I want to thank my students who encouraged me to write and collect these stories that I usually mention to them briefly in class.

CONTENTS

Map of Syria

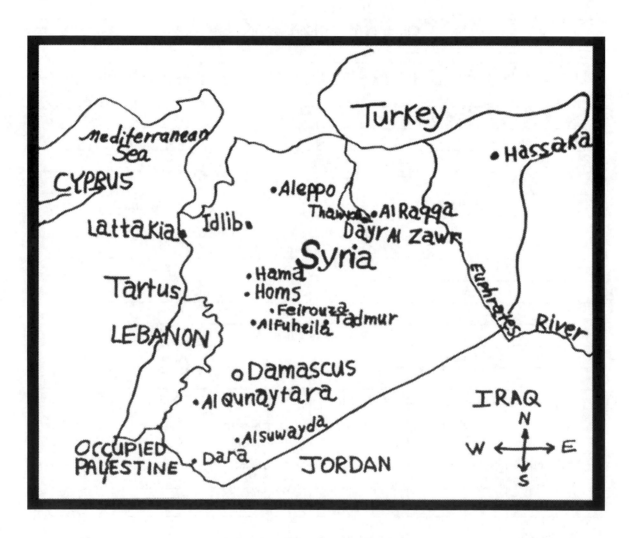

Map sketched by author

Tamara's Family Chart

Children from Oldest to Youngest									
Rammi	Nadia	Alice	Miriam	Maha	Anwar	Amira	Tamara	Faddi	Nabeel
↓			↓		↓		↓		↓
Son	Daughters				Son	Daughters		Sons	

↓

Parents

↓

Father: Baba (Rez)	Mother: Mama

Paternal Grandparents

↓

Grandfather	Grandmother (Sitti)

Aunts and Uncles					
Uncles			Aunts		
↓			↓		
Majeed	Elian	Shaddi	Huda	Mona	Lina
	Hend: Wife	Maryouma: Wife	Father Karim: Husband	Tanios: Husband	Gabriel: Husband
Children		Children	Children	Children	
Kamal		Amer, Samer, Zafer	Maher and Najwa	Yasmine, Feisal, Salem	

Cousins in Syria					
Awatef	Sanaa	Zeba	Amer	Samer	Zafer

Cousins Who Come to The USA							
Yasmine	Maher	Kamal	Feisal	Salem	Najwa		

Introduction and Background

I spent my childhood living in a very small village called, Alfuheila located about twelve miles southeast of the city of Homs in the center of the country of Syria. The climate was very similar to that of Southern California, with a nice warm weather in the summer and often, pleasantly mild winter. Sometimes though, when the weather in the winter was cold and harsh, everything in our daily lives became a hundred times more difficult, especially when we had snow. We did not have any paved roads other than the main road that lead to the connecting cities. Therefore, it was either dusty in the summer, or muddy in the winter. This made it very difficult for students who had to walk to school, for farmers to accomplish their tasks, for venders to travel back and forth to the cities to buy their supplies, and for women who had to spend many hours cleaning their homes from the mud and dirt.

Everyone in our village was of Christian descent, but we were surrounded with five Muslim towns. We all had our own elementary schools, but only our village, being the largest, had a junior high school where we converged: Alfuheila Junior High School. We all had to follow the same curriculum except for religion classes. The students from our town had Christian religious studies and the rest had Islamic religious studies. During recess, lunchtime, before or after school though, we never spoke about any religious issues and we got along beautifully, but one thing was very clear. We knew we could not have gender relations with each other and we could not intermarry. It was an unwritten rule and everyone in town respected and followed it then.

In junior high, we wore navy blue uniforms that looked more like military gear with white shirts and matching caps. We all walked to school in our village, but many from the surrounding villages came by bus, on motorcycles behind their fathers or other family members, or rode their own bicycles. We were in school from 8:00 AM to 2:00 PM and attended six days a week.

Our day off was Sunday and we all had to go to church, which was located in the center of the village. My friends, cousins, siblings and I were all involved in church activities, including singing in the church choir. I did not like going to church much because I could not understand anything the priest used to say. He spoke in Syriac, a Middle Aramaic language, which was used by Syriac Christians it was spoken between the eighth to the eighteenth century. Beginning in the eighth century, the Arabic language started developing thereby replacing Syriac, but it did not completely disappear. There are still some people in Syria and other parts of the world who speak it, and many clergymen still use it in Church sermons.

We knew how to recite all the religious hymns, but none of us really knew the meaning of any of them. We sounded great, though. I even became one of the main singers in school festivals and big patriotic events. This gave me a boost in self-esteem and a little bit of popularity among my peers.

I grew up in Syria between 1964 and 1978. At that time, most people in our town worked in farming. They depended on the harvest of crops as their main source of income, but also raised cattle and chickens to have an additional financial support while waiting for the harvest. Everyone in town had a piece of land enough to build a house and plant some fruit trees, and extra land for their other crops like wheat, barley and other types of grains. Some families had more land than others, and their land size depended on how the land was originally divided. Some families inherited a lot of land from their ancestors, and some did not because the inheritance was divided among the males in the family. In some cases, people received the title for the land from the government for land that they had worked for generations, which belonged to no one or to the state. My father was an only son, so he received all the land from his father.

My father was sixteen when he married my mother who was then nineteen years old. This was not common in our culture. Men usually married girls up to fifteen years younger than they were. In my father's case, my grandparents needed more help with the farm and with the house chores since my grandmother had developed a rare disease that left her paralyzed from the waist down.

My mother was a very smart, wise, and healthy woman. She did very well in school and had many talents in way of vocational work where there was potential for more income. She was also beautiful and came from an important family. Her grandfather, was the mayor of the town, then her father, and then my uncle took over and remains mayor until this day. All this made up for the fact that my mother was three years older than my father. They also knew they could depend on her to take on the responsibility of not only helping my father grow up faster, but to take care of the farm and bare many children to later help them, too.

My parents were engaged for a year when my father was only fifteen. On his wedding day, he had been playing Gulli (marbles) with his friends and my parents had to call him in to get ready for the day's events, which included his literally getting bathed by all his friends and dressed by the best man.

Even though my parents had an arranged marriage at a very young age, they grew to love and respect each other a lot. They had ten children—four boys and six girls. I was the sixth daughter. Growing up in a small town on a farm, we all had to share the responsibilities around the house and on the farm. When school was in session, most parents would let their children focus on studies and even cater to them when they had exams, and adult children would help them with everything. But, when school was out, kids would have to help with collecting the crops, taking care of the cattle and doing house chores.

Collecting crops could include picking almonds or grapes and packing them in bags or wooden boxes, or harvesting the barley and wheat and piling them up for the threshing machine to process them by separating the sticks from the grains. The part of the process you were told to take part in depended on your age. But you had to do something. Some of us had to lead the cattle to the main town shepherd or grazer so he could take them all to the green fields far away to graze. One of my older sisters and I often did that and used to sing all the way to the other side of town. Every family painted a spot on their sheep using a different color so that when we went to pick them up at the end of the day, we could recognize them. Many times we brought home the wrong sheep and other people did the same, but we knew whom to take them back to. We had a system in place that we followed. It sounds complicated, but we knew what to do.

Everything on the farm required physical work, and nothing was that simple to accomplish, but you just did it. Everyone else did the same thing, so we could not complain. My family had a chicken coup with thousands of little yellow chicks that quickly grew into big white chickens. I loved to play with them when they first arrived as little chicks, but the smell was horrible inside. I guess after a while, you got used to it.

Often, when we came home hungry from school, we would not see my parents at home, so we either scrambled some eggs or ate some homemade plain yogurt spread on pita bread with some sugar on top of it. Sometimes, one of my eldest sisters would come home, get a chicken, kill and pluck it, and then get it ready to make some chicken soup we called Yakhni. It had the chicken, the broth, sautéed onions and garbanzo beans, and we ate it with rice. Other times, we would come home, and my mother would have our favorite food, which required a lot of work. It is called Kibbi (made with ground beef and cracked wheat and stuffed with onions, ground beef and fried pine nuts).

Actually, when we looked around the farm, we had sources of food everywhere, from lamb, to chicken, to rabbits, to fruit trees, to grains (Now we call this organic foods), yet we were, as I recall, a poor family. In many peoples' eyes though, we were considered rich because we owned a lot of land, but I remember our family struggling to make ends meet. Some years the harvest was really good and we were able to buy many more things that we would not have otherwise, and other years, we just had to make the best of a bad situation. I guess we didn't have much money because all the ten kids were eating up all the profit! I don't know how they thought having many kids helped. By the time we were old enough to help, our parents must have had to spend so much money, and endured a lot of hard work to raise us.

The hardest thing for me when I was living on the farm was when my father used to wake us up at three in the morning to walk in the cold, and sometime ride on a rented tractor to go collect the crops. We had to do that early before the sun came up while the stems were still dewy (wet or moist) so the sticks would not crack. Often my father would hire extra people from the surrounding villages to help us. If they were late one day, it was not going to be a productive one, and this meant that the following day we would have to wake up even earlier. Once I told my father that my leg was hurting so I could avoid going with them, but I ended up doing more work at home. Oh well. I tried, but my parents knew all the tricks from all the kids who had tried before in so many creative ways to avoid work.

Even though I have many memories of when things were very hard on the farm, I also have many pleasant childhood memories. We had many happy events such as weddings, which would last seven days of partying, and kids were allowed to stay up as late as they wanted because all the weddings were held in the summer. There would be dancing and singing with many ritualistic activities that we enjoyed such as the Henna of the bride and groom, and pre-wedding bridal ceremony held by the bride's parents. We also had big church events on holidays such as, Christmas and Easter where we had games that were hand-made. We set them up in the center of town for all the children to hang out while the elders went around paying visits to all their close friends and family members. Other major events that happened in town were the many school festivals for patriotic holidays like Independence Day where

I used to sing, and many of us would be involved in some kind of musical or comedy play created and directed by my wonderful teacher Shamsa. Anther wonderful memory I have from the farm is when I used to play with my friends on the school playground when school was not in session. We often invented our own games because we did not have any special toys other than the ones we created ourselves from scrap we found around the house. But the memories that always stand out are those times when I simply hung out with my sisters and we did the house chores together while listening to the radio and memorizing songs for popular singers like Um Kalthoum, Farid Al Atrash and Abdul Halim Hafez. I also loved and still love the singer Wadee Al Safi who sings beautiful folk songs that anyone can relate to. I can still recite many of the long songs I learned when I was as young at ten years old standing next to the huge mulberry tree, which was in the center of the courtyard of our humble house, and listening to the radio inside my grandmother's room where my older sisters were washing dishes or preparing food.

Kids in general, in our town, were free to wander anywhere and play wherever they wanted. It was very safe to be out anytime of the day because everyone knew each other and everyone was protective of each other's kids. I guess you could say that the whole village was raising us. Most of the time our parents were out in the fields and we did not have to ask anyone for permission to go anywhere. As long as we did our homework or house chores (this was checked by our older siblings), we were free birds. In fact, my sisters wanted us out of the house to keep it clean and to also hang out with their friends without us bothering them. They also had to prepare food for the whole family and for when my parents and the other workers returned home from the fields.

During the year, my mother would help with the grafting of the fruit trees, which required a lot of skill that she had acquired from my late grandfather who died before I was born. My father would have to cultivate the soil to get it ready for seeding, and it would get very windy and dusty in our town during that time. As a result, he hurt one of his eyes badly that he had to travel to Palestine to have surgery done on it. There was a well-known eye surgeon that we had heard about. We had some relatives there and they hosted my father for a whole month. Unfortunately, he never recovered from the injury and became legally blind in that eye. This made it much more difficult for him to handle things on his own, especially as my oldest brother had finished school and gone to work in Thawra, a city which was a few hours drive from our town. My other older brother was in school in the city of Homs with his twin, my fourth eldest sister, and my younger brothers were too young to help. This is when my uncle in the USA heard about how all of us, including my other uncles and aunts, were struggling to make it. He had decided to send us petitions to be able to immigrate to the USA and be free from all the farming and the hard physical work that we had all endured. For a few years, my parents were waiting for their turn to come so we could migrate to America. One day, they received the news.

CHAPTER 1

ANTICIPATION: THE NEWS

I still remember the day when I heard loud screaming and laughter coming from our house as my friends and I were playing Bayour (a game played with a wooden stick and a short dowel sharpened from both sides) in our elementary school playground, which was near our house. It was Sunday, April 4th, 1978. My parents had just received news that they finally got their immigrant visas to come to the United States. My uncle Elian, who had been living in the USA for 15 years, had petitioned for all his brothers and sisters to come and be close to him and his wife as they were never able to have children of their own. My mother, Aunt Huda, Aunt Mona, Aunt Lina and Uncle Majeed all received the news at the same time.

It had been a long time since anyone from that town left to go to another country. So, it was a huge deal, especially because five big families would be leaving the village soon.

All my friends and I decided to abandon our game of Bayour and go to my house to check things out, and when we got there, it seemed that the whole town had come to learn more about the news. Some people were crying and others laughing, but my mother simply sat there trying to take it all in as she answered many questions that visiting women had. My father was busy serving ahwi murra (bitter coffee in Arabic), which was commonly served on special occasions, whether happy or sad. It usually took a long time to make since one has to roast the coffee beans, boil them in water, let them sit for a few hours, separate the liquid, heat it again and then pour it in a special thermos. At least this is what I remember Baba (father in Arabic) doing. *I had watched him make it many times.* The smell of the coffee had filled the whole courtyard.

I stood there with my group of friends patiently waiting for the candy and chocolate to be passed around. This was another common thing to do in our small town for any happy occasion like news of birth, graduations, baptisms, weddings, Easter, Christmas, formal engagements, or when men came back from serving in the Army. This was one of those occasions, and Mama had made trays of Baklava (a Syrian type of desert made with puffy pastry layers and filled with ground walnuts and sugar and garnished with ground pistachios), and bought tons of chocolates and sugarcoated almonds and many other types of candy, which were all being served on special platters with gold trim on the edges and beautifully hand-painted in the center. We only used them on very special occasions.

We could see the candy boxes being passed around to the men first. We knew that women came second, and then whatever was left over, went to the children. This was an unwritten rule that all kids knew even when it came to food, especially when we had guests over. I was thirteen years old at the time and loved candy, but when one of the boxes was finally in my hands, I was not interested in eating candy anymore. I suddenly got sick to my stomach and wanted to lay down somewhere, but there was literally no place to do that. My parents only had two big rooms. One was dedicated to receiving guests during the day. It had four long sofas, four side tables that fit perfectly in the four corners, and Mama's (mother in Arabic) beautiful Singer sewing machine by the door. By night, the room was turned into my parent's bedroom where they threw a huge mattress on the floor, which was covered with a hand-made rug from wall to wall and had been passed on to us from great grandparents. The mattress was filled with sheep wool as all the other family mattresses, which were made by Mama and Grandma.

The other room was a living room by day where we all hung out, did our homework, crocheted, knitted, played, did crafts, told stories to each other and in the evening, watched a little bit of television as we had nothing except a funny comedy show at 6:00 PM and after that, it was the news. By night, this room was turned into a bedroom for all ten siblings. Believe it or not, I looked forward to bedtime. I was never scared and my sisters always took turns telling us stories. Some they made up and others they had heard many times from older family members. I wish I could remember some of those stories to tell them to you. Maybe some day I will ask my sisters to retell them to me.

I asked my friend Awatef, who was also my third cousin, to let me go to her house and lie down for a bit because I could feel an anxiety attack coming on. Usually, my sister Mara would make me feel better no matter what the issue was, but this time, she was busy making tea for the women. She stood hovering over a big Rakwi (stainless steel or copper coffee pot with a long handle) in a small room that we used to call, Gurfit Sitti, (Grandma's room).

My paternal grandmother, for as long as I could remember had been bedridden and lived in that room. Grandma used to crochet and knit a lot, which kept her occupied. It also brought joy to her when she finally finished a sweater or a blanket that she would give to anyone in the family who was having a new baby.

We also used Grandma's room as a kitchen because it was the biggest room in the house. Of course, all the cooking was done outside in the courtyard so as to avoid fumes going to my grandma. She liked being in that room because she always had company. Every time somebody wanted to eat or cook, she would talk to them, but sometimes I avoided going in there because I did not want to pick up her poop (I know it was mean of me, but I was a child then and did not understand why I had to do that). Whose ever turn it was, we had to take the special bowl to an outdoor bathroom, which was a hole in the ground with four walls and a door that did not have a lock. We all had to help with that because my grandma was not able to stand up at all. She had a rare disease at a young age, which paralyzed her from the waist down. Even though we all had to help with feeding her and cleaning after her, I think the person who helped the most was my sister Maha, who was very compassionate and helpful to the whole family. My sister Amira also helped, but not as much because she had to do a lot of other chores around the house.

My Grandmother passed away when I was in fifth grade, and even though I never connected with her, I was very sad that day and the teacher told me I could go home early, which was the greatest gift you could give to any student, except for those few people who absolutely loved to be in school. I was not one of them then.

My cousin Awatef agreed to take me to her house, which was empty because everyone was at our house. She asked me why I was so sad and not feeling well. I could not answer her. It seemed that everyone in town was so excited for us. America was considered a dreamland for many and most people did not think they would visit it in their lifetime. In our case, we were leaving as legal residents. That was even a bigger deal.

"You know Tamtam? (My nickname with my friends) I am really happy for you. I can't believe you are all going to America. Are you going to write me letters?" Awatef cried and smiled at the same time.

"I don't want to go." I reluctantly responded.

Deep down, I really wanted to come to America, but I did not want my cousin to think that it was easy for me to leave her and all of our friends and relatives. She played with my hair, which my sister Maha had just washed, and it smelled good because we had just started using a shampoo that smelled like gardenia. Before that, we only used Saboon Ghar (soap made from bay leaves) for our hair and body and it did not smell as good. In fact, I hated it because it was a big bar, and it used to slip out of my hands when I tried to use it.

"Wake up, wake up." My sister Amira was yelling. I had fallen asleep on a small mattress on the floor at my cousin's house. My sister pulled me by the hand and said that I had to go home because everyone had to help with cleaning up the house after all the guests left. My part was to put all the teacups away and carefully place them in a wooden box, which was lined with red velvet material, for the next special event.

At the time that we received the news of leaving the country, some of my brothers and sisters had already been married and were living in a city called Thawra. I do not remember much about my three older sisters' weddings, though, other than images of the white dresses and some beautiful clothes that were made for my sisters by Mama who also designed and made clothes for many people in town.

I was thinking that if everyone in town seemed to want badly come to America, then my older sisters and my brother Rammi would really want to come with us. Mama was saying that they could not come with us for some reasons that at that time, I did not understand.

Being the youngest daughter of six, I did have more time with my parents and a little bit more attention from my older siblings, but I often got the short end of the stick. For example, I always got the hand-me-downs. I wore clothes worn by all my sisters. Also, when Maha and Amira finished house chores, they were able to go out with their friends until night time, but I had to stay in the house with my younger brothers and sometimes, when my older sisters came to town to visit, I also had to babysit their kids. I can tell you one thing. I was going to watch Mama make clothes so that I could make my own new pieces, and I was determined to grow up fast so that I would be able to go out with my friends like my sisters did.

I would often watch my mother cut up pieces of fabric from here and there and make me, and my sister Amira some dresses to wear on Sundays. Mama was a great designer, who had taught herself how to make clothes by watching other women in town, but became more professional than most. I loved the red dress she made for me when I was seven years old, which was made from an old skirt my sister Maha had worn for years. The dress was so short, but I loved it for some reason. I wore a pair of white shiny leather shoes with it, which belonged to Amira when she was seven. I felt like a grownup.

All my five sisters also learned from Mama how to sew, but Alice had actually gone to school for a year in the city to train in Homs with my Aunt Lina's husband, who was a professional tailor. His name was Gabriel and I liked him very much because whenever he saw me, he was very nice and always gave me money or treats. He and my aunt Lina had been unsuccessfully trying to have children for a long time, but now they thought coming to America would help them see good doctors and they were very hopeful that they would be able to have a kid one day.

I constantly watched my mother sketch, cut and sew. I started practicing making dresses for my doll, Salma, whose body I had made out of cloth and stuffed with wheat germ and rice. Sometimes I wish I still had it because I remember how it gave me comfort every time I held it close to me.

Maybe one of these days I will try to make a similar one to give to a future granddaughter or something.

Mama and I were talking one day, as I helped her record the measurements of this big old lady who only wanted my mom and nobody else to make her dresses. Helping Mama keep records of people's measurements was my favorite thing to do because I was able to actually spend quality time with her. It is also one of my earliest memories of writing things down and actually enjoying the task. I felt very important and took pride in my work as I organized all the names, age, and body measurements of all the clients in a very neat notebook. I would also modify the measurements if clients had gained or lost weight when they came to get fitted again or when they came back for other garments.

When the client left, Mama started sketching the design of the dress so that she wouldn't forget what the lady asked her to do, *but I would always put the final touches on all the sketches because I loved to draw just like my mother.*

Since we were talking, I took the opportunity and asked about how old my sisters were when they got married. I was curious. She answered me with a little sadness in her face that Miriam had gotten married at sixteen. "Alice," she continued, "got married at eighteen, but I really wanted her to finish school and become a fashion designer. She was so talented and learned so much from me, and Gabriel. She used to help me a great deal." I could see her hiding the tears that came down quickly down her tired face. I wanted to reach and wipe the tears for her with my little handkerchief that I always had in my pocket, but she had already wiped them with the corner of her shirt.

"Mama, what about Nadia? Did she also get married young?"

"She was eighteen and her husband was twenty-eight. She lives in Thawra, close to your other sisters and your oldest brother Rammi."

"Are they coming with us to America? I mean, are we all going together? I want us to see each other more mama. I have not seen my sisters in a long time." I cried.

I had so many questions, and my mom seemed to finally have time to talk to me. This was one of a few conversations I had had with my mom where she did not have a million things to do.

"No, no. They cannot come with us habibty (my love). They are married and cannot be on the papers." I did not really understand the "papers" part much, but she clarified that, "the petition states that only single children who are under twenty-one are able to go with their parents. Once we become American citizens, we will send for them." She assured me.

"You know Tamara, all these dresses I am making? I will not get paid for them. I want to make dresses for all the older ladies in town for free so that they will remember me for a long time." Mama looked happy and proud telling me this.

"Mama, you are always working so hard to do things for everyone, but not for yourself. I hope when we go to America you will be like a queen. Free! Free from farming, sewing, taking care of a thousand people and from the ugly smell that the chickens make. You know how that makes you cough all the time, ha?"

Mama smiled at me and I felt like she finally validated my words, and that also made me feel very mature and grown. "I think you should have been a queen, Imme (Mommy in our village dialect)" I added. I saw her have a bigger smile, and for the first time since I was little, she caressed my hair and my cheeks, and tears gushed from her eyes again.

I was thinking that when we came to America, we would finally have time with my parents as I missed sitting in my father's lap and drinking Mate (an herbal Argentine tea that we always drank in a ritualistic setting). My parents would not have to work in the fields all day and come home and do more work. I was thinking that we would finally have clean clothes, take showers when we wanted instead of once a week, we would maybe have some toys and our own beds, which we had never had. We had to put many mattresses next to each other to fit all ten children in one room. I was thinking we would finally have our birthdays acknowledged as they did on T.V. I was thinking we would simply have an easier life, and once and for all, my parents would rest from working on the farm while we worked and took care of them.

CHAPTER 2

FAMILY ISSUES: PREPARING FOR THE TRIP

The day of departure came sooner than we thought as my parents started packing all the belongings that we were going to bring with us to America. I saw my Mama carefully wrapping soup bowls that we had kept for many years, and China plates and small Turkish coffee cups as well as tea kettles of all sizes. I was wondering why we would bring things like that since in America they had "everything" according to what my uncle said in the letter. When Maha asked why we were taking so many things with us, Mama told her that they did not want to burden my uncle Elian when he found a place for them to live. They wanted to spend as little as possible on items that they already had. They packed blankets, sheets, rugs, decorated pillowcases, doilies that my sisters and I had embroidered or crocheted, and many more things.

We only had one big brown suitcase, which Rammi used when traveling back and forth to Thawra where he worked as a manager of a government-owned pharmaceutical warehouse. Since the suitcase was not going to fit much, Mama, who was very creative in solving problems, sewed rectangular-looking bags like suitcases and decorated the edges with gold twisted cords, the kind you use for furniture or curtains, to be more presentable. She carefully, and in her own special way, packed all the big items like blankets and bath towels in the bags with all the expensive plates and cups inside them so that they would not break. She then asked my father to move them to the courtyard where Maha and Amira tightly sewed the mouths of the bags. As they were sewing, they sang beautiful songs in unison, and I observed and listened from afar and tried to sing with them. I knew all the words to most of Um Kalthoum's (a very famous Egyptian singer) songs.

I had actually sung on stage in special patriotic events that we used to celebrate in schools, and the whole town would come and watch. I even sang on the same stage in town with a popular young singer who was a friend of someone there. His name was George Wassouf and he is still a well-known singer all over the Middle East and many parts of the world. I don't think he would remember me, but I still brag to my friends about having been on the same stage with him twice.

"Tamara, what are you doing there? Come and help me pack your brothers' clothes!" Mama lovingly yelled. Suddenly, she started humming songs that she used to sing to us when we were little. I do not know how, but I remembered the words to those songs too. Mama was so shocked when I uttered the words to the song. "How? How do you know these words? You were really listening when you were a baby." She then laughed loudly as she threw herself aback.

"No Mama. I used to hear you sing them to Faddi and Nabeel." I smiled.

"I know. I know Tamara. I am just playing with you,"

I started packing some clothes that belonged to my brother, which were not really new or in good condition. However, we all got new clothes for the trip that year that we were going to wear when we traveled to America.

I really wanted to pack my own clothes, but there was not much to pack other than a couple of pairs of bellbottom pants that my sister-in-law, Mary had given me, which Mama had fixed to fit me. I did have some undergarments and some socks which were also old, a couple of dresses that Mama had made from other hand-me-downs, and three t-shirts that I got from my sisters after they had worn them a million times. I was looking forward to wearing my new clothes on the plane.

I thought to myself at that time, *"When I go to America, I am going to learn English and graduate from high school and then study to be a fashion designer."* I was sick and tired of wearing other people's old clothes. I wanted to have my own new pieces, and my own fashion style. Most of all, I wanted to be free of all traditions and rules and hearing "Shame on you for this," and "shame on you" for that. Everyone was so worried about what people in town were going to think or say about them. Frankly, I did not really care about anyone's opinion, except my parents', but I had to do what was expected of me within our small community. Most girls followed these rules, so we could not complain or protest much.

As we were preparing for the trip, people from the neighborhood were coming by to see what we were doing. They were curious as to what people did when moving to another country. "Oh Um Rammi, we are going to miss you terribly here," a beautiful, middle-aged woman cried to Mama. Everyone in town called Mama, Um Rammi, which means, Rammi's mother. In Syria out of respect people address grown-ups by the name of their eldest son. Other people dropped in, and soon the whole courtyard was full of people. Each group was doing something to help my parents move and organize the things that were left in the house.

"What are you going to do with all these items Um Rammi?" An annoying woman asked. I know she was annoying because none of the kids liked her and she always wanted to get something for free. Her name was Um Abdo.

"Oh my oldest son Rammi and his family will move back to town and live here until their papers are ready. They will follow us in the future Inshallah (God willing)." Mama answered Um Abdo with her usual diplomacy so as to not embarrass her for her constant nosiness.

My brother Rammi, who was thirty-two years old and married with three children, had to serve in the Syrian Army because he was no longer helping my parents. According to Syrian law, service in the army for males is mandatory unless one is an only son or is helping his family because of financial hardship. Since we were coming to the US, he had to enlist right away. My brother Anwar, who was nineteen then, was on our petition to migrate, but could not leave the country before he had served three years in the military. So my father had paid a taxi driver to smuggle him into Lebanon, a neighboring country bordering Syria. We were going to meet him there as our plane was going to make a short stop in Beirut, the capital of Lebanon, before leaving for France, our second stop before getting to the US.

Rammi was not happy, as he had to leave his job in Thawra, and his wife Mary had to come and live in the village to which she was not accustomed. She had been a city girl, and Rammi did not think she would know how to deal with farming or the town's people. In addition, Rammi's income was going to be minimum wage while serving in the military. They were hoping that the harvest from harvesting the crops would get them enough money to get by until we were able to send them money from the USA. Baba had sold all the cattle and the last batch of chickens so that he could have some cash for the trip. At Least Rammi's wife would not have to deal with that part of farming.

"Oh I feel so sad leaving this home and all my neighbors and friends" Mama told all the ladies who were standing around her, with tears in her eyes. Everyone loved and respected my parents, especially Mama. She always tried to help others in any way she could, and she was very hospitable. Everyone loved her. There was something special about Mama. Even though she was only a little over five feel tall and had a small body, when she walked into a room, she would captivate everyone's attention. She had so much confidence.

"When you get there and settle down, you must send for us Um Rammi," laughed Um Abdo, and all the ladies laughed with her.

"She can't send for you." I yelled from afar. "You need to be a relative. My uncle told us," I added. I was afraid she might follow us, and *"that would be a disaster."* I thought.

"Oh, I am just joking habibty." Um Abdo responded with an attitude. She knew I did not like her. Just a week before, she told me that I looked so dark that I must have been from a different father (of course I knew she was joking, but that was not funny to me). I badly wanted to tell her to leave our house, but Mama always taught us to be very polite to guests even if they were annoying. So, I kept quiet.

While we were all doing some work, we could smell food cooking in my Grandmother's room. Maha was doing a million things at the same time, as always. She was cooking Yakhni (chicken soup and rice) and Amira was baking bread as usual in the electric Tanoor (Tandoor or an oven-like apparatus used for baking bread) and singing to Um Kalthoum. The ladies were impressed with Maha, as she had just gotten married to the young man she loved, but everyday, she would finish all her own chores at her in-law's house and then come over to help us prepare for the trip. She was supposed to come with us, but having gotten married, she was no longer eligible. I think she was very sad because she was young, pregnant, newly married and, very attached to my parents.

I also felt sad for Maha because I knew it was very difficult for her. She would not be able to come to the USA for many years. I think her turn was going to take eleven years if a sibling petitioned for her and if my parents got their citizenship, then it would only take about six years. *Also, out of selfish reasons, I really wanted Maha to be close to me wherever I went. She was like a second mother to me.*

"We love your daughter Maha," a lady said. "We will take care of her. Don't worry Um Rammi," she added. This is when my Maha heard the lady, and she and Mama broke down. Maha was crying uncontrollably and then Amira started crying and of course I followed, but ran outside in front of the house and hid until things calmed down.

My brothers Faddi and Nabeel were always out playing with friends and cousins. They came running to the house and were very anxious about some news. They seemed out of breath. As it turned out, my cousin Manaf had just passed away due to cancer of the stomach. He was only eleven and was one of my favorite cousins. We used to play together all the time. We were all confused and did not really understand what was happening, but sadness filled the air that moment.

Mama's world turned up side down in just seconds. She changed her clothes and wore all black, and all the other women went home and did the same. Everyone met at my uncle Majeed's house. All the kids gathered outside and we listened to the women whaling, weeping and yelling, "Not fair. Why? Why?"

Each kid had an explanation of why Manaf had died and what the cause was. Some thought he ate something bad and others thought he had "worms in his stomach." Of course we did not understand the word cancer at that time. I just told them that it was his turn to be the next angel. It seemed to give me comfort to say that and all the kids felt a little better. I always thought of him as an angel anyway. He was always sweet, generous and willing to play any game we suggested. He never argued.

After the funeral, all my uncles and aunts got together and discussed the possibility of postponing our trip to America until forty days had passed after Manaf's death. In the Christian Syrian culture, close female family members usually wear black for forty days, and some for years, but in most cases, they hold a church service as a memorial for the dead after which women are then encouraged by the elders to change black clothing to lighter colors and gradually to brighter ones.

All five families postponed the trip until August. We were leaving on August 17, 1978 and my aunts and uncle Majeed were leaving a week after us.

That day came very quickly, and all I can remember is that many people were at our house again and there was so much crying, hugging and kissing.

I do not remember how I got in the car, but I woke up in my uncle Shaddi's house in a different town called Feirouza. Apparently, my parents had grabbed us out of bed very early in the morning. My uncle Shaddi had a big van, and was supposed to drop us off at the airport, which was in Damascus, the capital of Syria. We left very early in the morning after we had eaten a nice breakfast prepared by my uncle's wife, Maryouma. On the way to the airport, I counted eleven people in the van—I, Baba, Mama, my sister Amira, my brothers Faddi and Nabeel, my uncle Shaddi, his wife, and three sons, Amer, Samer and Zafer who were just going along for the ride. I was happy that they had come with us because they made the trip fun with all the recycled jokes that we all knew. We laughed anyway and acted like we had not heard those jokes before.

We had not been close to my cousins before, except when they used to come and visit my maternal grandparents for a few days every year in the summer. We really bonded on the way to the airport. I wanted to keep in touch with them after we came to the USA, but I never did.

Thinking back, I remember looking out the window watching and observing everything along the side of the road, as I had never really left the farm to go to a big city before, except to see the doctor once for our X-Rays to send to the Immigration Services. I was amazed at all the houses on the way and all the cars on the road. I had not seen more than three cars at one time in our village before that. Many people had tractors, but we did not, even though my father owned a lot of land.

All our bags were placed on top of the van, but when we went under this small tunnel, some of the bags that my Mama had sewn fell on the ground, and we all had to come down and help put them back up. Luckily nothing was broken, or so we hoped.

After two hours of driving, we finally arrived at the airport. My uncle seemed to have some connections there, because we were able to bypass some people and go all the way in to the main gate. An officer hugged my uncle, and I saw my uncle slip some money into the man's pocket. It was then that three little guys came and helped us put all the bags on the conveyor belt. Nothing was opened, and there were no questions asked. We all got on the plane and we were supposed to make a stop in Beirut where we would meet up with my brother Anwar, who was smuggled earlier into Lebanon.

CHAPTER 3

TOUGH GOODBYES: LEAVING SYRIA

We said goodbye to my uncle Shaddi and his family that day, and on the way to Lebanon, my brothers and I were amazed how such a huge airplane could float in the air. We could not even make our paper kites do that. We were having fun because the flight attendant gave us playing cards, coloring pencils, and apple juice, which we had never had before. On the other hand, my parents and my sister Amira seemed very worried about Anwar not being able to make it on time or if he was even safely transported to Lebanon, as we did not have a way to communicate at that time. Mama kept praying, "Inshallah (God willing) Anwar makes it on time." I was also mumbling that word hoping to help with the situation.

We arrived to Beirut within a very short time. The voice from the microphone said that we should stay on the plane; they were just picking up more passengers and would leave in an hour.

I remember my mother crying a lot. The flight attendant kept coming back to comfort her because we had told her what was happening, but to no avail. Mama started to panic when forty-five minutes had passed and people had started boarding. She kept looking at every man that boarded the plane. She didn't remember what Anwar wore, but kept saying, "I will recognize his long hair."

Anwar finally came up the steps, and of course, we were all relieved. He looked so relaxed in his handsome suit, which I had never seen him wear before. I think Alice and Mama made it for him. We were all wearing new clothes and new shoes that day.

The plane took off from Beirut Airport. Our second stop was going to be Paris. Baba said to Anwar, "We are relying on you to be our translator in France." Anwar had taken a couple of classes of French in high school. He laughed and told my father that he did not remember much of what he had learned in class. Amira had had a year of English, but that was not going to help much in Paris. My two younger brothers and I had not had any exposure to either language, except for maybe some letters of the English alphabet, which we learned from our older siblings.

We all enjoyed the airplane food and constant drinks that we could get just by pushing a button. We even asked for snacks and the flight attendants generously gave them to us. It seemed like we were the only kids on the plane, as we got so all the attention. This was more attention than we had ever received from anyone before. My parents were always busy with farm work, and the siblings basically raised each other.

At this time, it finally dawned on me: "if we had to go to the restroom, where would we go?" I kept seeing people walking back and forth in the aisles, but I had no idea whether there were actual bathrooms on the plane. The trip to Paris was going to be about six hours. I really had to go. I wondered about my little brothers and how they had held it in for so long. I asked Faddi, "Hey do you need to go to the restroom?" He told me that he had to go badly, but he could hold it till we got to Paris if he needed to. I was not brave enough to ask the flight attendant, so I asked Mama: "I really need to go to the restroom Emme!" I thought she was going to tell me that I had to wait.

"Oh My God! Of course you can go to that restroom over there. Here, I will take you." She grabbed my hand and looked very worried about me. My brothers followed us. "When you go in, make sure to lock the door with the latch above and drop the tissue in the toilet and flush it using the button to the left. I will be waiting right here." I could not process much of what Mama was telling me to do. I just wanted to pee. Was that too much to ask for?

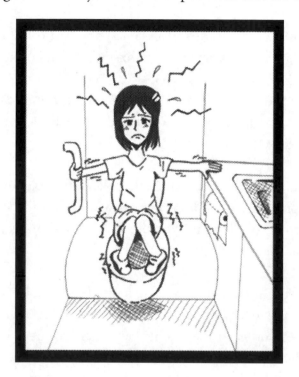

I looked at what was supposed to be the bathroom and saw a stainless steel round bowl, which looked like a seat with an opening in the middle. It did not look like our toilet in the village. It did not have a place for my feet. I wondered, "How do big people get on top of this toilet and try to balance themselves while pooping." I felt lucky being a tiny girl and I was very good at gymnastics, so I climbed on top of the toilet seat and did what I had to do. Even though I did not remember what my mother had just told me to do, I was curious and started pushing buttons, and one of them sucked everything in the toilet. I thought to myself. *"Wow! When I go to America, I am going to send some of these things to all my friends, my sisters Nadia, Alice, Miriam, Maha, and my brother Rammi."*

I heard knocking on the door, "yalla yalla Tamara (hurry, hurry Tamara). Your brothers need to go," Mama whispered from behind the door. Struggling to open the door, which you had to slide, and then open, I slipped and fell in the toilet. Of course my mother came to my rescue and my brothers were laughing so hard.

"What are you doing sitting in the toilet Tamara? You are supposed to stand on it." My brother Faddi said.

"No, no habibi (my love). You sit on the toilet seat to poop and you stand in front of it to just pee." Mama explained slowly. This is when I realized that I had done it all wrong.

Feeling victorious over Faddi, I said, "You idiot. Of course you don't stand on it. How are you going to balance yourself?" Of course I felt like the real idiot, but I would never tell a soul about this, except to you now.

My younger brothers and I had drunk so much Coke and apple juice and eaten so many sugary snacks that approximately an hour before we arrived in France we got very hyper and all wired up. We could not sit still. We were looking behind us at other passengers on the plane and people started to get annoyed.

I remember a young Lebanese couple (they had a different Arabic dialect) that looked like newlyweds and were trying to talk to each other, but kept getting interrupted by our jumping around and pushing each other in the isle. It made them so mad that they had to ask my parents to make us "shut up." My father calmly told them that he was very sorry and that we had never been on a plane before and that is why we were very restless and hyper. The young lady was polite enough and responded, "It's alright I guess. We only have about forty minutes left to get to Paris." She smiled and held her husband's hand tightly. I was wondering why she had to hold his hand. She was a big girl. "Was she scared?" I wondered. I was only fourteen and I was not scared at all.

Then there was an announcement, which came from the cockpit. It was in French as Baba said. My parents knew a little bit of French, which they had learned many years before when the French had control of Syria, but not enough to understand what the pilot was saying. After that, the announcement was said in Arabic because most of the passengers were either from Syria or Lebanon with some foreign passengers here and there. We were looking through the windows as the plane got lower and lower and finally made a safe landing, after which people on the plane started applauding the pilot for making it safely.

CHAPTER 4

THE LANGUAGE BARRIER: ARRIVING IN PARIS

We came out of the airplane and my parents seemed confused. "Where do we get our bags at?" Mama asked.

"Where's Anwar? Is he still on the plane?" Baba was worried.

"Oh no! He might still be sleeping. I thought he would follow us. My mother seemed worried again about Anwar.

I thought that he was supposed to be my parents' right hand. We were going to rely on him to translate to us from French to Arabic. I saw him writing poems most of the way there and the rest of the time he was sleeping. I think he was still angry with my parents for making him leave Syria and breaking up with the love of his life, a beautiful young girl who was also Amira's best friend. He knew he was never going to see her again. I had heard him and my parents fight many times before about this issue.

Suddenly, Anwar appeared behind us and said, "We need to go to Gate 12. We don't need to pick up the bags here. They will go straight to Los Angeles." He had apparently asked somebody about what we had to do next and really came through for us. My parents seemed so proud and followed Anwar as if he were a leader. I never saw my father walk so tall and so proud like he did at that moment.

"We have about three hours to wait for our connection flight. Just sit here and I will go and try to get us some food." Anwar was acting like a responsible young man and my parents could not believe it. They kept mumbling his name and smiling at each other. Amira was so quiet and seemed to be in her own little world, but she suddenly saw shops that had everything she had ever wanted! She started walking around, but my parents were worried she would get lost, so they sent me with her, as if I would know better. I think they knew that I would follow directions better as she had always been the rebellious one in the family.

Amira kept saying how she wanted to buy so many things, but we did not have any money.

"Ask Baba for money. I saw a bunch of money in his pocket when we were in Damascus airport," I told her. I really wanted to do anything so that Amira would smile again. She also seemed so sad all the way to Paris. I think she was already missing her friends.

"I am not going to ask Baba for money. We are going to need it when we get to America," She responded. Yes she was a rebellious kid, but she was always responsible for her own actions and owned up to her word. I respected Amira very much and looked up to her.

"Hey, do you want that?" Anwar's voice came from behind us. Amira was holding a beautiful silk scarf, which I am sure was very expensive. It was yellow, black, and white with flowers in the center (it felt as soft as the scarf Grandma used to have under her pillow, which she had gotten from her brother in Argentina).

"Yes, but I know I can't get it. We don't have money." Amira told him.

"Here, I will get it for you. Tamara, you also get something." He added. He said that Baba had given him some dollars when he went to Lebanon and he did not need it anymore. He had already bought some food and everyone was waiting for us to return to our seats in the waiting area.

Amira and I were very surprised about Anwar's sudden sense of responsibility and generosity because he had never been that close to us and never really paid much attention to anyone but his pen and paper, and his girlfriend.

I chose a lollypop, but asked if I could get some for Faddi and Nabeel because I knew they would get mad if we did not get them something. Anwar agreed and we went back to the waiting area where my parents and my brothers were patiently expecting us.

We seemed to be all bonding with each other as never before. We were actually talking together and discussing our trip and telling each other things that we had experienced so far on the trip. Of course, I would not tell them about the bathroom incident.

That day, I truly felt a lot closer to my brother Anwar because I saw a side of him that I had never seen before. He seemed to be genuinely sweet and caring. *Why was he always getting a bad rap from everyone?* I wondered. They used to say that he was very lazy and was always drinking and writing poetry. My father used to tell him to do something else that was going to make him some money—that poetry was not going to support a future family.

I loved Anwar's poems. I used to sneak in to his Kheimi, a tent that he and his friends had built in the middle of the almond groves. They would often party there, but also kept an eye on the farm from any wandering gazers who would let their sheep eat the leaves off of the fruit trees. I would open his notebook or journal book and read his beautiful poetry. Most of it was written to and about his girlfriend. I appreciated his writings and could not understand the negative attitude that the whole family had toward him for doing that. I guess he used to spend all of his time writing and they wanted him to be more productive and bring in some income to help the family.

It was now time to board the plane that would finally get us to our final destination, America. We were coming to North Hollywood, California where my uncle was going to host all five families for the first six months until we were all able to make it on our own. My uncle owned two liquor stores, one in Glendale and another in Eagle Rock, California, and supposedly, the adults were going to work there, according to his letters. That is what my parents had told us when we were talking in the waiting area of the airport in Paris.

CHAPTER 5

COMPLETE SHOCK: ARRIVING TO CALIFORNIA

After eleven and a half hours on the plane from France, we were all very tired, anxious, and excited to get to America. We were excited about meeting our uncle Elian and his wife for the first time, as they had migrated to America before some of us were even born.

We gathered together, making sure all seven of us were there. Baba stood there and counted us. This time, he was going to rely on Amira for translating from English to Arabic. *"I wish I could speak English to help my parents."* I thought to myself. Amira looked confident as always, pushing through the crowds of passengers and wanting us to follow. I always wanted to be confident and brave like her. She never feared anything. Even though she was only five feet two inches tall, she stood there like she was seven feet.

As we were following Amira, she was trying to read signs, which had arrows pointing to where we needed to go next. We got to the point where everyone was waiting to pick up his or her belongings. They were waiting next to what looked like a very large circular wide belt, which was going around and around, but nothing was on it.

"We need to wait for the workers to unload the baggage from the plane," Amira proudly explained to us. She had asked a man in a white uniform a little earlier. I was also proud of her for helping us.

I remember that day looking at my parents who looked so much in love even after thirty-three years of marriage. They observed Amira taking charge while Anwar stood behind her as if to say, "Yes, I do not speak English, but I am here to protect you in case anything happens."

I stood behind my little brothers holding their shoulders to make sure they did not stray away and my parents started spotting some of our items on the rounder.

"All the white bags have red ribbons on them." Mama said. "They also have your uncle Elian's name on them Yammo (term of endearment for sweetie). She yelled to Anwar, who was going to do the physical work of lifting all the heavy bags.

"I got it Baba. I got it. You just watch for the kids." Anwar now was in charge and Amira's job was going to continue later when we needed her to do any more translation.

"One, two, three, four, five, six, seven and eight," My mother counted the bags.

"We are still missing the big brown suitcase. We need to wait." Baba calmly said.

"Here it is." I said excitedly. I remembered that suitcase because I had seen my mother pack our things in it and had also helped her with it that day.

"Shatoora (Good girl) Tamara!" My mother smiled at me and I could see her two front teeth, which were covered with gold caps. She had gotten them many years before when she became a bride and they gave her such a distinct character. *Many women in our village had them. I do not know if they were used to protect the teeth or if it was a sign of wealth as some people thought, since not everyone could afford to do that.*

"Yalla yalla (hurry up). We have to wait in that line to get cleared." Amira yelled.

Baba handed all of our passports to the officer in uniform and smiled at him, hoping to easily get things done and move quickly ahead. The officer asked many questions, which Amira seemed to not understand. She seemed confused and uttered the word, "Arabic." I knew she meant we spoke Arabic. Very soon after that, another officer who looked middle-Eastern came and spoke to us in an Egyptian dialect. We could tell because we used to watch many Egyptian movies and listen to their music on the radio. Um Kalthoum, our favorite singer and whose songs we always sang or hummed, was Egyptian, as was Abdel Halim Hafez. It was still Arabic, but spoken differently. Of course, at that time, Baba took charge.

We were then told that we could pick up our Green Cards (now called Resident Permits) at the next window.

"You are now legal residents in California. Congratulations!" The Egyptian officer translated to us.

"You may walk forward and meet with your relatives outside. Just go around the corner to the right." He nicely guided us with a smile.

As we turned the corner, watching my parents and Anwar push three carts full of bags, I could see many people waiting impatiently for loved ones to arrive. Mama had shown us a picture of my uncle Elian and his wife when they got married. My uncle's wife, Hend looked so beautiful and everyone used to say how gorgeous she was. My uncle on the other hand, looked like an ordinary Middle-Eastern man.

Hend stood out from the whole crowd. She looked even more beautiful than I had ever imagined. She was tall, light-skinned and had a body of a twenty-year-old girl. *"Wow! I thought. "How did she marry my uncle?"* I saw him next to her. They were both smiling and looked very excited to see us.

The hugging and the kissing seemed to last an hour as my parents introduced all of us. My uncle's wife seemed very sweet and welcoming. I loved her right away. I was thinking she was going to be my best friend. I liked her style and loved her smile and how tears came down her face when she hugged me. I wished I could have been her daughter then. *"Why does God not give them a child?"* I wondered. *"They are such a sweet couple."*

On the way to my uncle's house, we were amazed at the number of cars on the "freeway" as my uncle explained. I was intrigued by the fact that one way, all the lights on the cars were red and the other way, all the lights were white. It was a captivating sight to us. My brothers kept saying, "wow! So many cars, Baba."

My uncle's house was in a city called North Hollywood. When we entered the house, it looked like a castle from fictional stories that we had read. We were lead to one room where we were all going to sleep, except for Anwar who would sleep in the garage with all the male cousins who were going to arrive later that month. The other bedrooms were assigned to my aunts and their kids. Uncle Majeed was going to sleep in the family room on a sofa bed as was explained by my uncle Elian.

"How are we all going to sleep in one room with my parents?" I wondered. Even though many of us had slept in one room before, we had never slept in the same room with my parents.

There was only one bed and I thought that it would be for my parents. But, soon Hend came in with some throw mattresses and gave us some sheets and extra blankets. After Mama finished arranging, the room looked like it could fit ten people.

"The showers are ready for you guys," Hend smiled.

"Oh, I have never taken a shower before," I said. I did not know how to operate it. I only remembered seeing something like that in an Egyptian movie, but this time, I was going to ask before I did anything. In fact, I was going to wait till my parents showered and then ask them.

Hend was very understanding and considerate, so she took Mama into the bathroom and showed her exactly what to do as I sneaked behind, observed and carefully listened.

When my turn came, I was very excited to not only experience taking a shower, but also to have water running on my body without someone yelling, "stop wasting water!"

We did not have enough water back home and we had to make do with just a few gallons everyday for the whole family. We could only bathe once a week on Saturdays. We had to be very careful since running water would alternate daily between the four areas of town, and if we ran out, we would have to wait until the next day or borrow from neighbors.

It was now my turn to shower! "Ya Salam! (Oh wow!) The water is nice and hot." I wanted to stay in the shower forever, but of course, the knocking on the door started and I had to get out so that the boys would be able to shower.

Dinner was ready and we all gathered at a huge dinner table, which fit twelve chairs. Hend had cooked what looked like a million things. Even though we were used to having feasts when guests came over, we never sat at a dinner table back home. *We used to sit on the floor around a big round Sidir (big tray usually made of aluminum) and ate directly from the platters, unless it was soup. In that case, we would share bowls.*

Hend had placed plates, forks and knives for each person along with a beautiful white napkin on each plate. This was all new to us as we lived on a farm and things were completely different.

We all sat and observed Hend and my uncle as they placed the napkins on their laps and grabbed the forks with their left hands and the knives with their right hands and started eating. My parents seemed to know what they were doing. *"I think they know this because they used to travel to the cities in Syria,"* I told myself. We all followed their lead, but not without trouble. I dropped my knife on the floor twice and Faddi could not use both utensils at the same time.

"Oh sweetie, just eat however you want to eat," Hend told him with a smile.

"Shukran (Thank you)." Politely and with relief, responded Faddi. And then Nabeel did the same thing.

In the morning, we woke up to the delicious smell of breakfast. As I walked out of the bedroom, all the curtains were open and I saw the most beautiful sight in the backyard: a swimming pool! I had only seen that in movies. There were many things in America that I had only seen on TV, but now I could have them or experience them. I did not want to eat. I did not want to sleep. I just wanted to live in the pool. Until that day, swimming in such a pool had only been a dream.

Later that week, Hend took us shopping at a place called "The Galleria" in Glendale and bought us new swimsuits. We had never owned swimsuits before and to imagine Mama and Baba wearing them was kind of strange to all of us, but they looked very cute when they finally put them on. It had taken my uncle Elian an hour to convince them that it was not shameful.

Hend ended up teaching all of us how to swim, even my parents. Of course, every one of us almost drowned at least one time in the process of learning. I personally almost drowned twice. Somehow, it was always Hend who came to the rescue or just happened to be there to save us. I really loved that woman. She was like an angel to all of us (we are still very close).

Two weeks later, my aunts Mona, her sons Salem and Feisal and her daughter Yasmine, my aunt Huda and her son Maher and daughter Najwa, my aunt Lina and her husband Gabriel, and uncle Majeed and his son Kamal arrived. Now the attention was divided as well as the food and snacks. The pool had more people in it, and Hend was no longer all mine as she had to entertain more adults and coach more children on how to swim

Things started to get more and more complicated by the day, as one can only imagine. The fun suddenly stopped with too many people in the house and many kids fighting and adults wanting to work, but not enough places in my uncle's stores for all to have jobs. Some worked at Uncle Elian's liquor stores, while others had to ask people in the community for work. Many issues come up and each person thought things were not fair for them. This of course, drove Uncle Elian and Hend crazy. They knew it was going to be a big responsibility, but they had not accounted for many things that were taking place. Of course, if you put many people in one house, even if they love each other to death, they are bound to fight. In this case, we were nineteen or twenty people in one house. On top of this, we often had many guests over, which made the situation a lot more chaotic and overwhelming for my poor uncle's wife, Hend.

Uncle Elian and Hend were very hospitable and generous, but could not possibly be fair to all. So, they were now arguing about everything, and I could not blame them. It must have been very overwhelming for them. *I thought that it must have been a lot more peaceful for them before they brought us to their lives. I almost felt bad for them.*

It was then decided that we would move out into a house that my father was going to purchase. Uncle Elian had suggested that we could all live together and the aunts would help us pay for part of the mortgage. Uncle Majeed, in the meantime, left his son here and went back to Syria.

My father used all the money that he had brought with him from selling part of his land to buy a big house in North Hollywood where we were still walking distance from my uncle Elian. It was OK for a while, but things got to be too much when my aunts' two husbands, Karim and Tanios and other cousins arrived later. We were again too many people in one house. The arguing and bickering started again and Mama and her sisters had many conflicts related to kids, food, work, friends, guests, and many other issues.

By the following year every family went their way and were financially able to handle their finances as they had more adults working by that time. We finally had the house to ourselves. We slept in a bedroom rather than in the family room on the floor next to ten other people. At last, we had some freedom to do and say what we wanted, and I am sure my aunts and their family members felt the same kind of relief.

We soon became very close again as we were when we lived in the village. We only had each other to rely on in a new country. We needed each other as a support system. Things began to go a little bit more smoothly.

CHAPTER 6

TOUGH TRANSITIONS: JUNIOR HIGH

It was June of 1979 and I had already finished one year in a Jr. High school in North Hollywood called, Walter Reed. Overall, it was a positive experience except for a few incidents.

On the first day of school, my uncle had set me up to use the school bus. So, we all woke up early and walked to the nearest bus stop. He and my parents had left me waiting with some other students and went to drop off all the other kids at their schools. Before I got on the bus, some girls were trying to talk to me, but I did not know any English to answer them. I saw that they were making fun of me because they were whispering to each other while looking directly at me, and laughing loudly after.

As I got on the bus, one girl tried to purposely trip me, but I did not fall. I went in the bus and took a seat next to a window. I liked to watch things as I rode any vehicle. I was daydreaming for a few seconds, recalling the day my Uncle Shaddi drove us to the airport in Syria when I sat by the window in the van and watched houses and building going by me. I had felt like we were idle and the objects were passing by us, and not the other way. The three girls sat right behind me and continued to talk to me, and when I did not respond, they started pulling my hair and roughly tapping me on the shoulder, "Hey, crazy girl. Hey bruja (witch in Spanish). Hey say something, stupid." They would not leave me alone. I was crying, but nobody seemed to care, except two identical twin sisters who seemed to be telling the other girls to stop what they were doing. They did not listen. This continued all the way to school.

When we arrived to school, I followed everyone and ended in some hallway. In addition to having puffy eyes from crying, wild-looking hair from being pulled every other way, I was lost and did not know where to go. I had no idea how the school system worked and had no relatives or friends there to show me. Everyone else seemed to be walking to the assigned classes, but I was suddenly alone in what seemed to me like a long hallway.

I could see from afar a huge silhouette of a big man coming at me and I got very scared. I did not speak one word of English, so I decided to wait and see what was going to happen to me.

When he dropped me off at the bus stop, my uncle Elian had given me his home phone number to give to the office in case I needed anything.

As the big man got closer, I saw him smile, so I relaxed a little. I was still afraid that he might punish me. He uttered a lot of words, but I did not understand anything except the word "class." I had learned it earlier from my uncle.

"No English." I responded nervously with my body shaking.

He motioned for me to follow him, but I was reluctant. I did not know where he was going to take me. We had heard about many strange stories that happened in America. But now an older lady was walking toward us smiling at me. She was trying to tell me something, but of course I did not understand. She then took me by the hand and walked me to the main office. She handed a paper to another student and asked him to take me to class, as I understood from her body language.

I followed the boy, but was very embarrassed that I did not understand English. He took me to room 101 where I met the teacher who was going to make my life at school very pleasant. Her name was Mrs. Lindgron. She smiled at me and took me to my seat and stroked my shoulder as to comfort me. I felt better and saw across from me a boy who looked like he could be Syrian. Later I found out he was from Iran and his sister Sara was also in the same class sitting across from him.

Amir and Sara spoke a little bit of English because they had been in America a few months before me. We used written Arabic and Farsi to communicate a little (both languages have the same alphabet and many cognates), but I needed someone to speak Arabic to translate to me what the teacher was saying.

For weeks, being in that ESL class and other ESL classes, I thought so many students spoke English so well. *"Why are they in this class?"* I wondered. *"They don't need to learn English."* As it turned out, those students were speaking Spanish all that time. I was finally able to distinguish between the two languages and had begun to understand many words in English. Every subject I was taking was ESL. I had ESL Math, ESL science, ESL Social Science and so on.

"School is so easy here." I thought to myself. *"If I were in Syria, I would have to study 10 hours a day to get through ninth grade. Here I am cruising right through it."* That made me very happy.

One of the classes that I had to take was called P.E. (Physical Education). I did not like that class because there were three big girls who teased and bullied me all the time, yet I could not complain as I wasn't able to express myself well. They would say, *"Hey freak. You don't speak nothin'? Hey crazy girl, say something."* Then one would pull my hair and the other would try to pull my shorts down. Then all of them would laugh loudly. I did not know why they picked on me out of all the other foreign girls. Or, maybe they picked on all new comers. I needed to find a friend who would defend me. I needed to learn English to defend myself. I needed to be more aggressive. I needed to tell someone about those girls. I actually needed many things and needed to learn everything. I felt so very naïve compared to students my age.

All the friends I made were ESL students from all over the world, but one girl was very special. Her name was Jennifer Beck from Korea. The other was Sara from Iran. We hung out at lunchtime and sometimes in the mornings if I happened to come to school early. I told them what was happening in my P.E. class and Sara informed Amir later. He said that if they did it one more time to tell him right away.

One day, all the students had put on their Gym clothes and met on the field. I did not understand the game, but we had a bunch of balls and wooden sticks everywhere. I kept hearing the word, "softball." But when I touched one, it was not that soft. I watched as a girl threw the ball to the other girl who tried to hit it with the stick, but missed three times. *I could do this easy.* I thought to myself.

"Hey, your turn at bat," the teacher yelled to me.

I had watched how they did it, so I got ready as I did back home when we played Bayour. It looked similar. The girl threw the ball and I hit it so hard, it went very far. I stood there enjoying the moment hoping that the three bullies would finally give me some credit and leave me alone.

"Run, run." They all yelled.

I did not know where or what direction to run.

"Run freak, run." One girl screamed. The twin sisters came to my rescue as they had done on the bus a few times before.

"Run that way to that white plate." They motioned to the right. "Go, go, go. Go to the second base. Continue, continue." They were all yelling. "Go home, go home."

"What?" I asked. I did not know what they meant by that.

The twins directed me again to come back to where I had originally hit the ball. Then everyone was hugging me. I had no idea what had just happened, but it felt good.

Earlier that morning, a bunch of girls had been pulling my hair on the bus and I was very scared of them. They had actually pulled out strands of my hair and were making faces as if to say that my hair was dirty, and they threw the strands on the bus floor. I looked down and it looked like half of my hair had come out.

That day, after I made a "home run," I was very happy, but dreaded getting on the bus. I imagined the mean girls with tattoos. They looked mean. Luckily, the twin sisters came and sat next to me and asked the girls to stop teasing and bullying me. I think they threatened to report them to the school authorities if they continued. I could understand a little more English then. That day, I was very grateful to them for saving me twice. I wanted to give them something to show my appreciation, so I had my mother prepare some Baklava Sunday night.

On Monday morning before my first ESL class, I ran into the twins and was going to hand them the bag of sweets, when suddenly a hand appeared and grabbed it quickly out of my hand. It was that big girl from my P.E. class. I was so angry this time and tried to speak English when she interrupted me, "I'm just kidding girl. I wanted to tell you that you did good the other day-you know, in P.E." She smiled and gave me back the bag.

That day was the last time anyone teased me for the rest of the school year. Even the girls on the bus found out about my home run and started to be nice to me.

"I love softball." I was thinking to myself. I guess it was because of it that people started respecting me, and because it reminded me of the Bayour game my friends and I used to play in the village.

CHAPTER 7

NEW OPPORTUNITIES: HIGH SCHOOL

The summer of 1979 was spent mostly in my uncle's pool and at many picnics that our church had. My uncle Elian was in charge of the St. George Church in Hollywood and my aunt Huda's husband, Father Karim, was the priest. So we all had to attend Sunday services and all other events. It was at times boring, but often fun when all the young guys and girls came to the events that related to the church. I used to make sure I dressed in my best clothes and stood out from the crowd. Do not ask me why I was like that. I could tell you a million reasons why!

In September, I started my freshman year at North Hollywood High School. My cousin Yasmine, who had taken a cashier's job at uncle Elian's Liquor store, decided to come back to school. We had been classmates back home and I loved her a lot. I wanted her to be with me so we could be stronger as a team against any bullies, but soon after we started, Yasmine quit school to go back to work. My uncle had wanted her to work and support her mom and brothers because her father did not speak English well to work there in her place. I was very sad to see her leave me. She later got engaged to a nice young Arab man from our community and seemed very happy.

By then, I had met a few students from Lebanon who spoke Arabic and we became good friends. I felt like I had a better support system now. I was still very close to Jennifer, and the twin sisters who kept close to me most of the time.

Because I had been telling Baba about the abuse on the bus, he was waiting for the right time to buy me my very first bike. Even though my little brothers could walk to the local elementary school, he bought them bikes too.

The joy of having a bike did not last very long because one week later, I went to the parking lot where I had left my bike locked. It was not there. It had disappeared. The chain was cut off and left on the ground. I had to walk about three miles to our house and then tell my parents what had happened. They had been worried and wondering why I had taken so long to get home.

Baba said he would buy me a better one and not to worry. "I will have your uncle talk to someone at the school to see what we need to do," he added. I was afraid he was going to yell at me, but I think he knew it was already difficult enough for us to adjust to living in America. He did not want us to worry about extra things. *I always thought Baba was a very sensitive, understanding and sweet man.*

The second bike was bigger and better, and may I add, more expensive. I showed off with it for a while and loved riding it around the neighborhood, and to visit my cousins and Uncle Elian and Hend. As luck would have it, the new bike got stolen from school the following month in the same way as the first one. Now, my brother Anwar had to start taking me to school.

That did not go well with him since he was not a morning person to begin with, and he had been working in a liquor store at night and needed to sleep in. Nevertheless, he still had to wake up early just to take me to school. I knew Anwar was not going to do this for long because he gave me a bad attitude every morning and he was always angry when I woke him up. I was thinking of possible solutions and asking around how I could spare my brother the headache of driving me to school.

This is when I heard about Driver's Ed classes to begin in the summer. My father agreed to the idea, but it was based on one condition. I had to find a job if I wanted to enroll in a Driver's Education class and if I wanted to get a car in the near future. Of course, I said, "Yes!" I was willing to do anything to spare Anwar the trouble of driving me to school and to drive a car. I could not believe that I was soon going to be able to drive a car. "Is it ever going to happen?" I wondered with much hope.

CHAPTER 8

FINANCIAL PRESSURE: MY FIRST JOB

Baba had heard from other community members that kids could get a job at a fast food restaurant at the age of sixteen. I was fifteen and a half then. This did not stop Baba from making me walk with him about three miles one way to the nearest McDonald's to get an application for work. By the time we got there, I was hot and sweaty.

We walked in and I asked for the manager. While waiting, I recognized some of the employees because they were students from my school. I knew a girl named Martha who was in my ESL Math class. I thought, *"I could do what she is doing. Her English is not much better than mine."*

A big man was looking at me from the kitchen area, but did not look happy for some reason. Then he came to the front and quickly said, "We do not have any positions open right now. Try next time."

I had to translate to Baba; *"They don't have a job for me now, Baba. The man said to try again next time."* I was actually relieved. I did not want to work. I was still not comfortable speaking English to people outside the classroom.

"Ask him to give you the application anyway." Baba told me.

"Mma may I get the application?" I stuttered and nervously asked and I did not think I had pronounced the words correctly.

"I SAID WE DO NOT HAVE JOBS RIGHT NOW LADY. DIDN'T YOU HEAR ME?" The mean manager spelled it out for me angrily.

"OK. Thank you Sir." I was scared. I did not like that big man. I surely was never going to work there, ever. I was crying on the way back to the house, but Baba kept telling me, "You are letting that man get to you. You need to be tough and try again. You will be denied things sometimes and you will be rejected other times. You will simply not get things to go your way some times. You may lose to others and you may fail in some things, but all these negative things should be lessons and opportunities to get stronger and wiser."

I listened and did not know when I stopped crying, but by the time we got home, I felt a lot better. Baba knew exactly what to say without getting all worked up. He was a very calm and patient man. He was very wise and had a photographic memory of everything and I envied him for that. *I had been struggling all my life with not remembering material that I had studied or even jokes that I had sometimes wanted to tell friends.*

The next day when I saw Martha, I asked her how she liked the job and also asked her if the manager was as mean as I thought he was. "Oh, he is real mean. He does bad things to girls." She spoke softly. She went on to tell me that he had gotten some seventeen-year-old girl pregnant and had her leave work to live with him and that he was also cheating on her with the new morning crew chief, another young girl.

I did not even understand the concept of getting pregnant or anything like that. Things like this were taboo in our small community in Alfuheila (our village), but nevertheless, it all sounded scary. How was I going to explain that to Baba? I thought that I should just never mention it.

Martha did say that she liked getting money from working and enjoyed buying things for herself and her brothers and sisters who were much younger. I wanted to make money too, but I still did not want to work, and definitely not with that mean man.

A week later, I had just walked from school and was extremely tired. Baba had been waiting for me and Mama had made me lunch on the go so that we would leave to go to McDonald's again. I complained and complained to no avail. Baba insisted that we go back and try again to get an application. "You have to be persistent, ya binty (my daughter)," he told me softly. "You must try again and again and again," he added.

I was still scared from the first time and shy to ask again for a silly application. I was hoping that a different manager would be there. I was praying all the way there. "Remember what we talked about the last time. You need to be strong. The worst thing that could happen is that he will say no again." Baba reassured me and tried to give me confidence. "If he says no this time, ask him when exactly we can come back. Put him on the spot. Get him to see that you are serious about working." He kept giving me advice, but I was still trembling with fear.

At the door, I just didn't want to go in. Baba slowly and softly pushed me in and held my shoulders from the back, "Go on Banoot (another word for little daughter)."

"May I please talk to the manager?" I asked a young boy in a green uniform.

"May I ask what you need to see him about?"

"I need an application for work."

"Oh, OK. I will get you one. Hold on a minute." His nametag said, "Greg." I recognized him from school. I think when he saw me he recognized me too.

"Here you go. Bring it back when you are done filling it out." He smiled. Greg sounded very pleasant and helpful.

"Why don't you try to fill it out here so we do not have to walk here again tomorrow," Baba suggested.

The boy was cute and I preferred to return the application to him rather than to the manager.

While I was filling out the papers, I saw many other students from my school working there, laughing and seemed to be having fun. This time, I was hoping to get the job. I really wanted to make Baba happy.

I was done filling out the application and as we approached the counter, I could hear the mean man's voice in the background. He was scolding a girl about coming late to work, as far as I understood from the conversation. I was scared that he would come and take the papers from me. So, I tried to get Greg's attention and motioned for him to come to me. *"Here you go. It is all filled out."* I handed the application to Greg.

"What have we here?" Lou, the manager, came up and asked with disgust in his face.

"This young lady turned in her application, Lou." Greg said.

"You are that girl from the other day, right? Who is this? Your father?" Lou asked.

"Yes, yes." I answered while shaking and sweating.

"I REMEMBER TELLING YOU THAT WE DO NOT HAVE OPENINGS NOW." He spelled it out for me, but not with the same anger as the last time.

"But Lou, you know Martha and Debbie quit." Greg interfered.

"Go check on the crew, Greg." Lou looked mad. "Give me that application. We will call you if we need you, OK?" He was not very pleased with Greg's involvement, but he also did not refuse my application. I was semi-happy because I did not have to come back again and beg for an application. I had done what I needed to do to get Baba off my back. Now, I hoped that Lou would never call me.

"See how it pays off to be persistent ya binty?" Baba reminded me.

Four days later, Lou called me for an interview. I put on my best clothes and asked my uncle to come with me to help translate if needed. My uncle Elian spoke English very well and had been living here for many years. Nobody could bully him. He knew all the laws and he knew his rights as a citizen.

When my uncle introduced himself, and Lou recognized him from the liquor store down the street (By then, Uncle Elian had bought a third liquor store in North Hollywood that he had shared with another family member). Lou seemed to be a lot nicer now. He shook my uncle's hand and said that he could stay with me during the interview. I was very relieved, especially after what Martha had told me. And now that she had quit, I had no idea what had happened. I could not ask her either because she had not come to school for three days.

My interview ended up being a conversation between Lou and my uncle about liquor stores. "I really like Tequila." Lou was hinting to my uncle to bring him a bottle. I was thinking that he was going to give me the job hoping that I would get him some alcohol from my uncle's store. Martha had also told me that Lou was an alcoholic.

"Ok, Tamara. You can start on Monday from 3:30 to 11:00 PM. You must get a work permit from school, though. You are not sixteen yet." He smiled. "Bring it with you on Monday, and by the way, as a student, you can only work 25 hours a week. You need time for homework," he added. He seemed like a different person.

Of course I was excited and also more confident that Lou knew I had people behind me who spoke English and knew the laws.

I was given an ugly green uniform made of polyester with a hat that looked like a clown's hat. The last time I had worn a uniform was in Syria where we had to wear military style attire to school. I hated those uniforms too because we did not feel like girls. I guess I did not like any kind of uniform because by then, I had worked very hard on developing my own fashion style.

They started me on French fries. I stood in front of the frying baskets all day, filling and emptying them. I was feeling tired and hot and was supposed to take a break for ten minutes. I was hungry from the smell and thirsty from the heat, but I did not know if I should ask for a drink and I did not have money for food.

"Here you go Tamera." Greg handed me a small drink.

"It's Tamara, not Tamera." I smiled at him and said, "Thank you."

"You can get a drink for free during breaks, but for food, you need to pay and you get 35% off." Greg explained. "But don't say anything; I will make you a delicious Big Mac." He whispered and told me to take an extra ten minutes and finish eating. Greg was such a nice guy. He knew exactly how I felt. I guess he must have gone through the same thing before he became the Crew Chief.

I was very thankful Lou was not there that night. Greg had said that Lou usually only worked till 3:30 and the supervisors or Crew Chiefs took over in the afternoons. He added that Lou also worked on Saturdays, which I hoped I would never do.

That night, I walked home by myself at 11:30 in the dark and was very, very scared. I was thinking, *"How did my parents not think about that? Why wouldn't they think of meeting me at least half way?* I also gave them the benefit of the doubt that they had to attend to my younger brothers and wait for Anwar to come back from work.

Walking on a main street, I noticed a car slowly getting closer to the curb and it seemed as though the driver was trying to ask me something. At first, I did not think much of it, but then when the man pulled over and opened the window, I got scared, but thought maybe he was going to ask for directions or something. He was trying to ask me if I wanted a ride. "No. No thank you." I quickly responded and started walking faster and at the same time, looking to see if I could get somebody's attention. The man started driving faster to catch up with me. This is when I saw another man coming out of a used car lot, which I had walked by many times before. I had often seen the same man at the place. So, I ran to him and told him that the other man in the car was "trying to do something bad to me." Of course, the guy drove off quickly, and the car salesman walked me to our house two blocks away.

I was thinking to myself that I was either a magnet for bad people, or I had the worst luck any human being could ever have. "How can so many bad things happen to me?" I wondered. I thought I was trying to do my best. I was nice to everyone. I helped everyone. "Where is that thing we call God?" I was so angry and scared that night. I will never forget the face of the man in the car.

I had made it home in forty-five minutes. Mama and Baba were anxiously waiting for me outside.

"Ahlan! Ahlan!" (Welcome! Welcome!). Both of them greeted me and hugged me.

"Go shower and change into your pajamas, Tamara. You must be exhausted." Mama looked worried. I had decided not to tell them what had just happened.

"Mama, Mama, Mama!" I screamed. "Come and see my legs." Just when I thought things couldn't get any worse.

"What's wrong?" Mama came running. "Shhhhhhh. Your brothers are sleeping."

I had not even gone in the shower yet. I showed Mama my thighs. They were swollen and red. I had been standing in that polyester uniform in front of the hot oil all night.

"Bring the toothpaste Rez." Mama cried. "This won't hurt. It will cool the burn down and you will be able to sleep better. Don't shower today." Mama suggested. I was now in pain and had some homework to do, but I was extremely tired. *I thought I would wake up early to shower and do my homework.*

In the morning, the swelling and redness had turned into blisters filled with liquid and I was really scared. My legs looked like I had come from another planet. I ended up not going to school, but that day I was scheduled to work. What was I going to do? I could not take off the second day at work.

Even though my parents were worried about me, Baba reminded me again to be strong and that in a couple of days, things would be back to normal in terms of my legs healing. I listened and went to work after Mama wrapped my thighs with a clean cut-up white cotton T-shirt that she had gotten from Baba's dresser. Mama always knew First Aid because my brother Rammi had taught her. She took care of many people in town and always had different medicine that Rammi would bring her from the pharmaceutical warehouse where he worked. I guess Mama was great a wife, a mother of ten, a farmer who took care of many fruit trees and plantations and helped raise thousands of chickens with Baba, a fashion designer, a nurse, and of course, a builder because she helped Baba build Grandma's room and later helped to turn it into a kitchen! Nevertheless, I was angry with her and Baba for being so naive as to let me walk alone late at night at the age of fifteen and a half. I could not understand that.

When I got to work that day, I was surprised, and disappointed to see Big Lou there. Somebody said that Greg had taken the day off because he was sick, and Lou had to cover for him.

"Tamara, I need you to go and clean the bathroom." Lou demanded. I did not know how to clean a bathroom and I did not know it was part of my job. "Ask Dirk where the cleaning stuff is." He added.

Dirk had been working there before I started, but was a very nice and shy guy. *"Can you show me how to clean the bathroom?"* I asked him quietly and with shame.

"You know, you are not supposed to do that. There is a cleaning crew that does that at the end of the night." Dirk whispered. "Lou is just testing you."

I was mad. I went up to Lou and said that I did not know how to clean bathrooms. *"I am to do French Fries only."* I continued, *"Dirk said that there are special people who do this job."*

The next thing I knew, Dirk was called and the scolding began. I felt bad and guilty for telling Lou what he had said. "TAM-MEERA." Lou yelled. "Come here. Follow me to the basement. We need to bring out some foam cups and other supplies."

I was afraid, but remembered Baba's words, "Be strong." I also remembered Martha's words, "He does bad things to girls."

"When I tell you to do something, whatever it is, you do it. Understand?" Lou grabbed me by the shoulders and shook me aggressively. He said many things, but I was fixated on his bulging eyes and scary-looking mouth and not really listening.

"DO YOU UNDERSTAND?" He often spelled things out when he got angry with any of the employees and treated us as if we were stupid.

"Yes. Ok." I started crying uncontrollably. I thought he was going to do something bad to me like what Martha was telling me. When he saw me crying and making noise, he started to calm me down and tried to put his arms around me. This is when I ran upstairs as fast as I could and went outside. I guess Lou was afraid I would tell someone there or maybe my uncle. He apologized so many times and told me that I did not have to do anything but fries. "After three months, I will train you to be a cashier. You will get paid more money, hon'. You are a good employee." He was patronizing me.

He was trying to bribe me to not say anything about what had taken place. From then on, I felt a lot stronger since I had something on him. I never told Baba because he would have made me quit. I wanted to continue working to help my parents and to be able to get a car.

After two weeks, I received my first paycheck, which was $113.00 after taxes. I got paid $3.25 an hour. I proudly handed the check to Baba. I had no idea what to do with it anyway.

I worked at McDonald's for eleven months and learned to speak English a lot better that year. I learned how to drive and got my license at sixteen after failing the driving test five times. Most of all, I learned that if I was going to live in America, I had to toughen up and learn a lot. I was going to start reading all kinds of books and ask many questions. I did not want to miss a thing. I wanted to be smarter and be more knowledgeable and I never wanted anyone to ever take advantage of me. Of course life is not as easy as that.

CHAPTER 9

DIFFICULT LESSONS: MY SECOND JOB AT BABA'S LIQUOR STORE

In May of 1980, Baba bought a liquor store from a family friend with the advice of my uncle Elian. Baba had gone back to Syria to sell the rest of his land to bring money so that he could secure a good income for the whole family. He also knew that soon, my brother Rammi and his family would come and we had to take care of them financially until they were strong enough to be on their own.

The store was called, Melrose Market and was located on Melrose Boulevard in the Middle of Hollywood. Anwar became the general manager and Baba was kind of the supervisor, but did not speak any English, so Anwar acted like the boss. It was fine with Baba because he wanted Anwar to feel responsible. Before that, Anwar had been working seventy hours a week at a family friend's liquor store to support our whole family. Now, he was his own boss. He bought a brand new car, a new house, which had six bedrooms and four bathrooms in Canyon Country for all of us. He even started buying us nice gifts, which we really enjoyed. Life was good.

I had to leave my job at McDonald's because Baba and I had to work the night shift at the store. Besides, I had to drive because Baba was legally blind in one eye and could not drive. Every day after school, I would get home, eat something that Mama prepared for me quickly, and then drive to Hollywood to work until 11:00 PM.

At first, it was exciting to be the cashier and to be the responsible daughter. I was helping my father in the family business. It was also exciting because we had three video machines, the kind they had in arcades and often when we did not have customers, my little brothers and I would play Pac-Man, my favorite game, Galactica and Centipede, some of the popular games from that time. But, as time passed, we had many major issues to deal with at the liquor store.

First, Anwar was working so many hours at the store that sometimes, he was not able to wake up early enough to go and open the store in the morning. As a result, I had to miss school to go to work. I was not of legal age to work by myself there, so Baba had to go with me. I was already doing my homework between customers, and was falling behind on all my assignments. Luckily, I had good teachers who seemed to understand my situation, and from time to time, I would bring them something special from the liquor store, or some home-made Baklava that Mama used to make, which was always a big hit at the school office.

The second problem was that we had started seeing drug dealers who shamelessly sold their drugs right outside the front door of the store. We were very scared to say anything and even more scared to call the police. We thought that if we called, they would know about it and do something bad to us. They often gave us little "baggies" (very small plastic bags that zipped) of things that seemed like either drugs or something that looked like it could be smoked. By then, we had learned so much about marijuana and other drugs from talking to customers, but none of my family members had ever tried any of that stuff before then. I think at one point, we had so many little plastic Baggies that we did not know what to do with them. Baba kept them in a box underneath the big brown paper bags where we also hid all the large bills.

One day, a couple of guys gave my brothers a little plastic bag of something and told them to take it home and try to smoke it. "It's real good," Roberto said. Roberto was about seventeen, but sold drugs near our store and around the neighborhood to support his family of nine siblings and parents. The guys were trying to bribe my brothers so that they would keep quiet about them selling drugs by the store, but they often had bad intentions. That night, when we closed the store and went home, my parents and I had gone to bed early, and my brothers Anwar, Faddi and Nabeel stayed up to figure out what to do with the bag without Baba's knowledge. Apparently, they had tried to smoke it because Nabeel, who was twelve at the time, came to my room screaming and telling me that Faddi, who was fifteen, was doing very strange things. They had been sharing a bedroom, and Nabeel had woken up to Faddi's punching of the walls and making holes in them. *How did we not hear all this?*" I wondered. When I asked him if he knew what had taken place earlier, he said that Faddi and Anwar had "smoked some of that stuff that Roberto gave them earlier at the store." I went to their room and could not believe what I was looking at.

Faddi was literally jumping up and down. His body seemed to be doing things on its own. At times, I saw his body almost fly all the way to the ceiling and drop back down. I had never seen anything like that in my whole life, not even in movies. Suddenly, he looked like he was choking. We were too scared to wake up Mama and Baba, so I called 911 hoping that if I explained to them what had happened, they would tell me what to do and I would not have to tell my parents. The woman on the phone told me to put a paper bag on his mouth and let him breath in it. She said that he was "Hyperventilating." She added that I should ask him to breathe deeply and rapidly into the bag. "This happens when people have anxieties, overdose on aspirin," No, no. I interrupted. I think he smoked something." She said that she was going to send the Paramedics. In a matter of minutes, Police and ambulance cars came, and a fire truck had followed. Suddenly, our front yard looked like a crime scene.

Since Anwar was older and his body was bigger, the drugs had not affected him that much. He had slept like a baby. Even with all the noise and my parents waking up, Anwar was still sleeping. Faddi had probably inhaled more, and it had really done some damage to him that night. It took six big officers and the Paramedics to hold him down.

The Police told us that they had to take him to the station, I do not remember why. On the way there, as they had explained to my parents later, Faddi started to wake up from that nightmare, and the officers turned around and drove him back home. Mama and Baba were very relieved. They were kissing Faddi all over while scolding him in Arabic about what he had done. That was a lesson to all of us about drugs. We were not in the village anymore, and we could not accept anything from strangers and not be as trusting as we were before.

We then told the Cops what had happened, and that none of us had ever tried any kinds of drugs before. They really believed us. "We have a whole bunch of baggies in the store that we don't know what to do with," I added. "We can show you. We can even give you all of them. We don't do stuff like this, officer. I swear," I cried. He said that they would do their own investigation the following day and take all the plastic bags for evidence.

A while before, Mama and Baba were shaken up badly as the officers took Faddi away. My parents or I had no idea what they were going to do to him at the station, and I had to translate, but lied and assured Mama and Baba that "They will bring him back in the morning."

As it turned out, the Marijuana had angel dust or a substance known as PCP. The Police had seen this happen to many people before. They gave my parents a big lecture about the need to be more attentive to their kids and to monitor their behavior and actions, and other stuff that I could not translate. We were all thankful that Faddi was fine and nobody was in trouble with the law.

In addition to all these issues we were facing at the liquor store, we often saw many people stealing, even in front of us. One time, a man just walked in. I knew him. He came to the store very often. He went into the beer cooler, grabbed two twelve-packs of beer, and as he was walking out, he said, "Thank you darling." He just walked out without paying, just like that. I was astonished at his action. I could not understand how he could do that when I knew him by name and knew some of his family members. I called out his name, "Hey, Jose. You didn't pay. Hello? Jose?" He did not even turn around.

Another time, a family of six walked in and started opening packages of everything and eating the contents. They had done this before, but it was usually only the children. I kept saying, "Excuse me Ms. You need to pay first." The older woman completely ignored me, and called more people to come in. It seemed like we had a whole tribe of them. Baba was in the cooler restocking some sodas and, I could not leave the cash register. I told the older lady that I would call the police, but she said to go right ahead. "By the time you call, we will be out of your hair honey." She had a very harsh voice like some women who smoke three packs of cigarettes a day. The lady was very calm as if she had done this a million times before.

In fact, two of the guys who were with them had once convinced my brother Anwar that they did construction work and that they could fix our parking lot to look better and be stronger when big delivery trucks drove in. "We will charge you half-price." One of them said. Of course, they did the work, which they finished in three hours. It looked good, but after a couple of days, it was cracking everywhere. They did not care when we complained. They had no license, and we had little knowledge about those types of things. They knew we could not take them to court, and actually kept coming to the store with their family all the time without feeling any shame.

I can tell you that day, the family ate more than they would at an open buffet, and they got away with it. When I called the Police, they came five hours later and took a report, but as always, nothing came out of it.

You would think that nothing worse could happen to a seventeen-year-old girl, and that I would be now wiser and smarter and would know how to deal with situations better. But you would be wrong!

One day, on a quiet Sunday morning, I drove to the store and opened it by myself. We had a regular customer named Johnny, who must have been about seventy years old, and would stand behind the counter with me when I did not have another adult at the store. Baba wanted to take Sundays off to go with Mama to church. We would compensate Johnny with cigarettes and a bottle of his favorite drink, Cuervo Tequila, a Mexican alcoholic drink.

That day, a young man walked in carrying a bucket and some cleaning materials like a bottle of glass cleaner, a sponge and a roll of paper towels. He asked me if I would let him clean and shine all the store windows for only five dollars. To tell you the truth, he broke my heart, and I had so much respect for him having woken up early to make a few dollars to support himself and probably his family. To make the story short, I agreed and told him I would give him ten dollars instead. He did not seem that excited, but said, "Whatever."

I would not be exaggerating if I told you that the young man worked for more than four hours, and the windows and doors had never looked so clean. I was very happy with the results, but Johnny kept telling me that he thought there was something wrong with that picture. "Why would he spend so much time here for five dollars?" Johnny asked me and kept wondering. "I've been around, mija (My daughter in Spanish), He advised me to be careful.

When Anwar and Baba finally made it to work, I showed them what a good job the young man had done and that he had asked for only five dollars. They were also pleased with the work. "I hope you gave him more than five dollars," Baba smiled.

"Of course I did Baba. I gave him ten dollars and a free soda." Baba was proud of me.

At 11:00 PM, Baba and Anwar closed the store, set the alarm, and went home. At 2:00 AM, we received a call from the Los Angeles Police to inform us that a customer who lived across the street from the store had called and reported some irregular activity. He had seen a huge truck with a few people loading boxes from the store.

Baba, Anwar and I drove there, and called the agent at the alarm company, who did not even know anything had occurred. Apparently, when the young man was cleaning the window, he had used a blade to cut the alarm wires in many places so that when he and his team came at night to rob the store, the alarm would not go off. That blew us all away, but the Police had seen this happen before, and that it was very common. I blamed myself very much for having been so naive as to be fooled like that, but Baba kept comforting me and said, "It could have happened to anyone. I could have done the same thing. We will just learn to be more careful next time." Baba always knew what to say to me to make me feel better.

To top all of these things, we often got robbed at gunpoint, which was the scariest thing that could happen when working in a liquor store. There were a few times when we were even robbed at gunpoint, also by people that we knew as regular customers.

There was this time when George, a regular young customer, who was like a friend to all of us, had come in the store earlier and bought cigarettes and a beer. Towards the evening, he knew that Baba was taking a nap in the liquor room (He had asked about him earlier) and put the gun to my face and yelled, "GIVE ME ALL THE MONEY, NOW, NOW, NOW." He called me names, which I cannot tell you. I was very scared and confused. *"Georgie, what's wrong with you? It's me, Tammy (my American nickname)"*

"Open the register and put all the money in a bag. I won't hurt you. HURRY, HURRY," he yelled.

"Georgie, why? We're friends." I pleaded, but he suddenly jumped over the counter and started dumping everything from the cash register into a big paper bag. He even took food stamps and employment and government checks that we had cashed for customers earlier in the day. He also reached in my back pocket and took whatever money I had, and jumped over the counter towards the front door and ran. I was actually happy that he did not see the large bills under the big brown bags.

I woke up Baba and told him what had happened. This time he was very worried and scared for me. "I will never take a nap again. Are you Ok ya binty? Did he hurt you? I can't believe Georgie did that. Are you sure it was him?" Baba had so many questions and so many concerns. I could almost see tears in his eyes.

We called the Police, but they came four hours later. While one officer was getting his notebook from the car, the other officer was whispering to me not to describe the robber precisely.

"This whole neighborhood is full of gangs and drug dealers. Things have really gotten worse. If we catch him, he may send someone to hurt you guys." The officer told me. I was shocked that the cop would say that to me. I thought they would try hard to find him and protect us from that ever happening again. But actually, they never caught any of the other robbers. Baba said that we had to at least report the loss to the insurance company because they required a Police report. By now, I had started **fearing** coming to work, and I really needed to focus on my studies anyway, as this was my senior year.

I had experienced being robbed at gunpoint once before when I covered as a cashier at Uncle Elian's liquor store for a week when I was sixteen then. The box boy, who was over twenty-one years old, was restocking the beer in the big cooler when a tall man on roller skates came in the store waving a gun and demanding that I give him all the money. He suddenly saw Saleem, the box boy, coming out of the cooler and commanded us to both go inside the bathroom. He pulled me by my shirt and also took Saleem by the hair while still holding the gun near my right shoulder as he grabbed me tighter. Then he closed the bathroom door. We could hear him dragging kegs of beer and placing them behind the door so that we could not come out. I thought he was going to start shooting at us, but we heard a lot of noise, which sounded like glass bottles breaking and things being thrown around. We also heard coins dropping on the floor. When things calmed down, we were too scared to come out, but we heard someone call loudly, "Hello? HE-LL-OOOO?"

We yelled, "We're here, we're here. Please help us."

The customer came and removed the kegs, and we got out safely, but the store was very messy and things were broken everywhere. We then called the North Hollywood Police and made a report. They said that a similar robbery had happened at another store a week earlier. Nothing came out of the report or the so-called investigation.

After the incident with George, I did not trust any customers. We all became very vigilant and were not as nice as before to people.

We had been anticipating the arrival of my oldest brother, Rammi and his family soon. We were all hoping that Rammi would finally give us a break at the store. We were all tired, especially I.

CHAPTER 10

WORKING FOR INDEPENDENCE: MY THIRD JOB, MY NEW FRIEND, AND MY FIRST BRAND NEW CAR

Think about your life or the lives of people around you, and answer the following questions. Record your answers in the boxes below.

By March of 1982, close to my graduating from High School, my brother Rammi and his family had come (with a petition from his in-laws in Oregon) to stay with us and then we were all working at the store. The situation there got a little better at the store since we had more people to monitor, and thieves would think twice about taking action. Nevertheless, we still had other issues to deal with.

Even though the store was generating a lot of money, things had to be divided among more family members now. Baba had wanted Anwar to look for a wife. He thought if he got married and settled down, he would stop wasting his hard-earned money on dating, going out with his friends and his latest hobby, gambling at the horse race track.

Of course, now that I was speaking English well, Baba suggested that I leave and find a job in "retail or something," as he put it. I was happy to leave that area and the liquor business, but mad because I knew all the customers and Baba needed me there to communicate with all the sales representatives and delivery people when Anwar was not available. Rammi's English was not that good, but Baba said that Rammi needed the job more because he and his family had been talking about moving out on their own. All of us living together had created conflicts between Mama and my sister-in-law, Mary. She was a very pleasant woman and I thought of her as my own older sister. But our experience of having too many family members living together had taught us enough to know that it did not work.

I graduated from high school in May of 1982 and got a job at a newly opened clothing store in Encino (in the Valley) on Ventura Boulevard. I do not even remember how I found out about the position. I just remember being interviewed by a lady outside in front of the store.

Throughout High School, I only had friends at school and never outside. I had gone to school and worked. I had done my homework and run errands for my parents. I had also taken them to family functions, weddings, baptisms, funerals, visits, doctors' appointments, the office of Social Services and the Social Security office. You name it. I did it. But I did not have any real friends. It was not like my parents left me any time to do anything for myself. I basically went through my teenage life and early adulthood without having had much fun whatsoever, except for the two times I had gone with some people from McDonald's to the beach, and some church activities. Oh, yes. There was one other time when Baba had sent me to John's Market, an Armenian super market in Hollywood, o buy a box of bananas and a box of tomatoes for the store. It was about 10:00PM that night and I had run into a group of guys and girls from church. They were all dressed up and were going to Aladdin nightclub for the night. I do not know how, but they managed to convince me to go with them "for a short while." I ended up staying more than forty-five minutes and Baba was getting ready to close the store. When I got to the store, Baba had an angry look on his face, but he seemed relieved to see me.

The day I began my work at the clothing store, I met this beautiful girl who had the sweetest smile. She was also a trainee. We were both working the cash register and we really hit it off. She made me laugh about anything. Then we started spending our breaks together and shared many secrets including the fact that I had never had a boyfriend.

"Really? Never?" She shockingly asked. "I think I have had six so far," she added.

"I was in love with my first grade teacher when I was ten, if that counts." I tried to make her laugh.

"I need to fix you up with my brother. He is a nerd, but you can fix that."

"Oh no. I can never go out with an American guy. My parents would kill me." I closed all doors for her so that she would never try to fix me up with him.

"Actually, I want to fix you up with my brother Anwar. He always says he loves girls with green eyes. Maybe you can make him forget his girlfriend back home." I told her about their love story. She jokingly said that she would take it as a challenge and make him "forget that his girlfriend back home even existed." I was laughing so hard, but I was not sure whether she was serious or not.

Anwar came to pick me up from work one day. Earlier that week, I had forgotten about putting oil in my Chevy Chevette (a little four-cylinder car), which I had gotten from Anwar when he bought a new car. Actually, I had no idea I had to check the water and the oil regularly. I just knew to fill up gas, and some guy at the gas pump would usually ask me if I wanted him to check the oil or water. Sometimes nobody was out by the gas pump to help, so I filled up gas by myself. Apparently, I had not had the water or oil checked for a long time, so the engine or transmission had burned.

I had been driving to work one day when I saw smoke coming out of the hood of the car. I pulled over and walked to the nearest phone on the freeway. While I was calling my brother, I saw the car explode right before my eyes. It went all up in flames. I felt so lucky that I was not in it.

"Why do these strange things happen to me?" I wondered. I wondered about many things in my life and how unlucky I was so often when I was working so hard and had all good intentions.

Anwar had been driving me back and forth to work for a couple of days and he was going to pick me up that evening.

Anyway, my friend had insisted on meeting Anwar.

I cannot describe the reaction of both of them to you. Imagine how my car exploded. Well, the sparks between Anwar and my friend were even more intense. They hit it off right away and started dating. It was no longer a challenge of fun for my friend, but she was falling in love. Sure enough, in a few weeks, my friend had affected Anwar positively and he wanted to marry her. My parents loved her and started buying her stuff, as they would do for a new bride back home. She loved that and could not understand their generosity.

"Why are my parents Ok with boys doing what they want and marrying who they want? Why are they so strict with the girls?" I asked myself. They always justified all my brothers' actions, but all the pressure and responsibility of "maintaining our family's good reputation" fell on our shoulders, the girls. I never understood that.

One day, to show off in front of his new girlfriend and to show his appreciation to me for introducing her to him and for having helped him at the store so much, Anwar surprised me at work with a new Special Edition Chevrolet Camaro. His girlfriend's father had also bought her one, so they both had gotten "a good deal," according to Anwar. I could not believe I had a brand new car like that. Just five years before, my cousins, Zeba, Sanaa and I had stolen my aunt Hilani's donkey from the stable to go for a ride and pick some grapes from my parents' groves, which were two miles away from the village. Now, I had a brand new car all to myself! I was in Heaven! I did not want a boyfriend or anything else. I just wanted to fill up the tank with gas and drive non-stop anywhere by myself with the music blasting to the maximum. At that time, I wished my friends and cousins from Syria were with me. It would definitely be different and more interesting than riding a donkey.

Later, when Anwar asked to meet his girlfriend's parents, she said that it would not be possible.

"I have to tell you something, Anwar," She nervously said. I was standing next to her and knew that she was going to talk to Anwar about the situation.

"What is it?" Anwar looked worried.

"Well," She hedged. "We are Jewish . . . and my parents are very clear about my dating only Jewish boys," she cried.

Of course, Anwar had never asked about her religion. He did not care.

"Once they meet me, they will change their minds. You'll see," Anwar laughed and assured her. "Besides, my parents might also have an issue with your being Jewish, so we just have to be smart and convince both families that we love each other and there is nothing they can do to separate us." He was very much in love with her and was willing to do anything. At least that is how I saw it.

Unfortunately, even after Anwar met the family, things did not go well for many reasons. There were the cultural and religious differences, the language barrier between my parents who did not speak any English and my friend's parents, and the ethnic background as well as the socio-economic status. Her parents were very rich and Anwar was just a poet and the son of a liquor storeowner. At that time, I thought Anwar was still in love with the girl from the village because he stopped fighting for his relationship with my friend.

After that, I stopped communicating with my friend so as not to bring heartache to my parents and Anwar, and also to avoid any negative friction with my friend whom I adored. I wanted to keep the beautiful image of our amazing and innocent friendship, and our so-called adventures together.

When Anwar and my friend broke up, I officially had zero friends again. I now only had my sister Amira to visit and talk to all the time when I was free.

CHAPTER 11

FOLLOWING MY DREAM: FIDM (THE FASHION INSTITUTE OF DESIGN AND MERCHANDIZING)

All my life, I had wanted to become a fashion designer, but my parents wanted me register at Los Angeles City College (LACC) and major in Business. Uncle Elian had told them that it was a good major because "the USA is built on business." According to him, I would have a good job once I graduated and would be able to make "tons of money." That made my parents very happy and they pushed me even harder to stick with the Business major.

I had finished one semester at LACC, which did not go very well. The following semester, I decided to transfer to Los Angeles Valley College (LAVC). I wanted to be closer to home and to my sister Amira's hair Salon in Van Nuys, which Baba had bought for her when she got her beautician's license after she graduated from high school.

I came to see Amira everyday. We were both also taking a P.E. class at LAVC. We played tennis together and went out to lunch often. She always paid because I was not working then and she was making good money doing hair. That is when I met Rick, one of her clients, who also owned a dry cleaning shop next door to her. He told me about the Fashion Institute of Design and Merchandising (FIDM) down the street in Sherman Oakes. I had been talking to him about school and how much I had hated my business classes and how I had dreamt of becoming a fashion designer like my mother. They called my mother a seamstress in town, but I think she knew more than any designer.

That day, I decided to go and inquire about the program and the tuition. I had to take a drawing test where the director gave me five sheets of paper with nude bodies drawn on them. I had to draw fashionable clothes onto the bodies to show whether I had potential. She was blown away with my drawing and sense of fashion style. That gave me a huge boost of confidence. The last time I felt that confident was when my English teacher. Ms. Ramirez, in high school praised me for my essay in which I had to describe an important person in my life. I had written it about my mother and it made her cry.

I remember filling out papers from FIDM for a student loan, which had to be read and signed by my parents, as I was only nineteen years old then and needed a co-signer. I was not going to tell them, so I took the application to my sister's salon and filled it out there. I also signed for my parents. I knew how they signed because I had faked their signature on many of the school notes in high school when I needed to cover for Anwar at the store. Besides, my parents did not speak English and I could have written anything on those notes.

Now that I was going to change my school and my major, I had to tell my parents. I was sure that they were going to find out sooner or later. With the help of my sister, we went home and explained all about the FIDM Fashion Design program to my parents. I told them that it was what I really wanted to do and that I had been thinking about it all my life. Mama's face lit up because deep down, she knew I had it in me to be an excellent designer. After all, she had taught me everything I knew. Amira tried harder to further convince them and they finally said that as long as they did not have to pay anything extra, they were fine. I was not going to tell them that it was going to cost close to thirty thousand dollars plus expenses, but what I did tell them was that the school had a job placement program and they could find me a job right away, which made them very happy. "I can pay for my expenses and maybe I will be able to get financial aid," I tried to make the deal more attractive.

In 1984 I began my journey at FIDM. I loved what I was doing, the people around me, and I was excelling at designing and pattern making. I was surrounded with fashion and fashionable people. When we visited the garment industry downtown Los Angeles I would feel like I was in a candy store. I also made many friends because we saw each other at least six hours a day, we shared ideas, we ate lunch together on the huge balcony in the then known as the Lincoln Savings building because all the bottom floors belonged to the bank and the two top floors were for our school. The big FIDM branch was down town Los Angeles where I was going to transfer once I finished my first year.

I had always loved clothes, shoes, jewelry and everything related to fashion. I soon started making my own clothes and turning old pieces into new ones as Mama used to do when we were in the village. Amira was a hairdresser and I was going to be a fashion designer. We often dreamt of having our own style consultant agency.

We shared everything. I would let Amira wear my new clothes and she would always try out new products or new styles on my hair. Sometimes I was her model at hair fashion shows at big conferences. We used to also model in front of the mirrors at the salon and dress alike when we went out to eat. People would always look at us and smile, and often make comments like, "You are both so pretty," and ask us questions like, "Where are you from?"

We loved the attention, and we loved saying proudly, "from Syria." Many people would ask where Syria was. One time we told this guy that we had met at a fast food restaurant that Syria was a city in Texas, and he said: "I knew that. I was going to say that." We later laughed so hard and made fun of him.

"Where is your accent from?" Some people would ask, and we would make up stuff like, "we are mixed-Syrian, French, Argentines and American." We had become a bit cocky.

"Wow! How is that? That is very interesting. An older woman said to us at a Denny's restaurant.

"Our dad is Syrian and French and our mom is half American, half Argentine." Amira explained. Of course we were just having fun because those questions were asked often and we were getting bored with giving the same answer. We did get in trouble once when a man said that he also spoke French. He was very excited to speak to us. "Oh our dad speaks it, but we didn't learn it," Amira quickly told him and we got ready right away and left the place.

My favorite part was when we ran into two actors that we had recognized from some T.V. show that we had been watching. I think it was called, "Eight is Enough." We went up to them and asked them for their autographs. I do not remember their names, and I wish we had kept the autographed papers that we had gotten from the restaurant owner. It was very exciting to be that close to known T.V. personalities. They tried to get our phone numbers, but of course, we would never do that as we were still very scared of my parents if they ever found out we were talking to any men.

Amira and I shared many things. One day, she told me that she had been secretly dating an American man. She said that he worked in the film industry. That sounded fascinating. I envied Amira for her courage, and adventurous life style that she had always had, even when she was living back home.

Amira was my hero and role model because she was the first to do anything that was unconventional in our culture. She was the first in our family to graduate from an American high school. She was the first, and youngest girl in our community to have her own hair salon. She was also going to be the first girl in our family to have an interracial relationship.

Before that, many families had come to my parents to ask for her hand in marriage, but she always refused to even meet with them. She was never the traditional type, and coming to America made her even more non-traditional. By the age of twenty-three, she had become a vibrant, courageous, beautiful, smart, rebellious woman who knew exactly what she wanted and went after it without much concern about what people said.

As for me, I was then twenty-one, and the family thought I was already "an old maid." Since they could not convince Amira with the idea of marriage, they now focused on me. People had been asking my parents for my hand in marriage for a few years now, but like my sister, I had been resisting the whole idea and wanted to experience falling in love and marrying the person I wanted. My three oldest sisters had married my brother Rammi's best friends, and Maha had married one of my brother Anwar's friends, who often hung out around our house. This was one of the many ways people got to know each other in the village.

CHAPTER 12

REUNITING:
MY SISTER MAHA COMES TO VISIT

In 1985, my sister Maha came to the USA to visit us. We had not seen her in seven years. She was still waiting for her turn to migrate to the USA, but she had missed my parents terribly and could not wait any longer. We were all very excited about her coming. I was especially ecstatic because I had so many great and happy memories of her. She had always been there for me.

I loved having Maha around again. *I remembered when she used to take care of me when I was younger.* I wanted to do things for her, too. She brought Clair, one of her two daughters with her, and they both brought a lot of joy to the family. Because of them, we started doing special activities like picnics and going to theme parks. We also had more family gatherings, and I got to show off all my designs and drawings, which Mama had displayed on all the walls upstairs. Every time someone came over, she would give them a tour and show them my drawings. She was very proud of me, and I think I reminded her of herself when she was young.

One day, when my parents and Maha were talking about me, she had told them that I was now old enough to get married, and that there were a few guys in the village who had expressed interest in marrying me. They had apparently sent messages with her and some of my brother Anwar's best friends had sent him letters to convince me to go back to Syria to possibly marry one of them.

"They don't even know me." I told Maha, but I knew well how things worked in our culture. I still got very angry, though.

"They know you come from a good family. They have also seen your pictures at my house." Maha responded.

"I am not marrying anyone from there, but I want to go back and visit," I said. I had not thought about it that much before that day.

I had been working at a hardware store where FIDM had placed me for the past year, and loved my job. I had become the head cashier and felt very important. I loved all my co-workers, especially the manager, Jim who was the owner's son, because he allowed me to work around my school schedule and was always supportive of me. I did not want to leave the job to go to Syria, but I had decided that I would. I told my manager that I would come back to my job after three months.

I was planning to spend the whole summer with my sisters and friends and come back to finish Fashion school. I was planning to become a famous fashion designer and make a lot of money to help my whole family. I was planning to open a big clothing store when I graduated so that when new immigrants came from Syria, I would give them jobs. I was planning to buy an apartment building to host new comers for the first six months until they were able to be on their own. I knew how hard it would be for them if they had to stay with family or friends. I was planning to travel to Paris, Italy, New York, and the Middle East to go to

Fashion shows and bring back ideas to Los Angeles. I guess I had many plans, goals and many dreams, but I was confident that I would accomplish most of them.

In August of 1986, I went back to Syria with Baba, and we had a great first month as I was having the time of my life with my old friends. Some of them had already gotten married and some were still looking for good husbands. We held parties everyday and we stayed up late and reminisced about old times. I had missed being a free bird on a farm. We did not have many rules there. *"Why do we have so many rules in America?"* I wondered. Even though they call it the "land of the free," I had felt a lot more free on this farm. I could not understand that. I often wondered if we really came from a "farm to freedom," as they used to tell us back home.

That summer, in June of 1986, my life turned up side down.

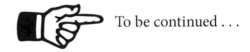 To be continued . . .